Christianity:
the Challenge of
a Changing
World

Tom Molnar

Apple Valley Press

Christianity , the Challenge of a Changing World

Copyright © 2012 by Tom Molnar

Includes *A Quick Look at Heaven*

Apple Valley Press

ISBN 978-0-9766952-0-2

What's Happening to Christianity?

> Is worldwide Christianity in decline, or is it changing and growing?

> How are men and women personally affected by the new culture?

> Has religious belief been transformed by the popular ideas of Darwin, Freud, Hugh Hefner and others?

> Have all the scientific advances of the twentieth century reduced the need for faith?

> Does Christ continue to make a difference in the modern world? In what way?

Preface

Polls show declining attendance at Christian churches in Europe. In America, many young adults are not part of any Christian congregation. Church schools close each year, and some of the great cathedrals of Europe exist more as museums than places of worship. Yet in other places, in other countries, Christianity is strong and growing. What is the state of Christianity today, the two thousand year old faith tradition of Europe and the Americas?

Our society is changing and so is religion. Culture has been transformed. The pattern of human life, though never simple, has been altered, probably forever. For thousands of years, most people went to bed soon after the sun went down and rose when the sun came up. Then, late in the nineteenth century, and more commonly in the twentieth, major changes began to affect our lives. These changes have become ever more pervasive in recent years.

It all started with the magic of electricity. Besides lighting our homes, electricity runs our computers, televisions, charges our automobiles, cell phones and changes our life dramatically. No one could have guessed that human life would be so transformed in less than 100 years.

Does the message of the man from Galilee resonate with the current world? Are his words timeless? Faithful Christians would answer in the affirmative. Certainly, people of different religious persuasions consciously feel a personal relationship with Jesus Christ. Prayer is far from dead. Nevertheless, in religion as in everything else, there is little doubt that the new age has changed our way of thinking, affecting us far more than we realize.

The future stands before each of us. We make choices as individuals, families, and as nations. However, our choices are never entirely free. We are affected by our family, our environment, and by our civilization. This book will examine the impact of the new culture on our beliefs. It will also look at how some remarkable scientific discoveries are beginning to change how we view the world. An appreciation of the powerful forces acting upon us may very well enable us to act with greater freedom. It may change the way we think about God. At the very least, it will give us a better understanding of how we are personally influenced by the changing world in which we live.

Chapters

1. The rise of faith and the decline of belief.

2. The coming of the modern era.

3. Five concepts that changed Western thought.

a) Popular secular attempts to explain the world.
b) Major religious world views.

4. Has Christianity changed our way of life?

5. Did Christianity civilize society?

a) Killing for God?

5. Is TV influencing our beliefs?

6. Where Christianity is rapidly growing.

7. Unanswered questions

8. Belief in God and science.

The rise of faith and the decline of belief

When Christ was actively preaching his gospel, in the backwaters of the great Roman Empire, few knew the man or his message. News didn't travel as it does today. Consequently, only those who heard him speak, or whose neighbors spoke of him knew anything about Jesus. He was, however, troublesome to the Pharisees of his day.

Nevertheless, the ordinary people liked what he said, and his increasing popularity turned the crowds away from the Pharisees' monopoly of religious practice. The chief priests and scribes sought a way to put him to death, but they were afraid to arrest him as he taught surrounded by crowds in Jerusalem. Then a traitor, Judas, went to the chief priests and offered to lead them to Christ during the night. After his arrest and hasty trial, the scribes and pharisees succeeded in persuading a reluctant Pilate to sentence him, after rousing an early morning crowd to cry for his death.

Contrary to popular belief, Christianity did not at first grow by leaps and bounds. Paul and the apostles had successes and failures in their missionary activities. Many Jews became Christians, but the Jewish religious authorities retained the upper hand in Israel. Jewish religious officials were directly responsible for the martyrdom of at least two of Christ's apostles.

In Rome, things fared little better for the nascent sect of Christianity. Many Romans were won over to the new faith, but once the gatherings became large enough to be noticed, the persecutions began. The major persecutions started with Nero in 64 AD and ended with Diocletian and Galerius in 311AD. Fortunately, they were not continuous, and many years, and even decades, separated one persecution from the next.

Nero began the first major persecution when he blamed Christians for starting a great fire in the merchant section of Rome. Many at the time accused Nero himself of starting it, especially as immediately afterward he had a colossal palace built on the site of the ruins. Terrible tortures were inflicted on Christians to make them confess to a crime they didn't commit. Nero had some of them dressed in animal skins and fed to wild dogs. Others he had crucified and burned on the grounds of his palace, their fire consumed bodies becoming torches to light his gardens.

Nero had become emperor at the age of seventeen thanks to the machinations of his mother, Agrippina. She married the emperor, her uncle, and then apparently had him killed so her son instead of his would be the successor. At first, Nero ruled satisfactorily under the direction of his advisors. In time, however, he became infatuated with his own singing and poetry as well as with a former slave girl. He killed his wife and then had his own mother killed when she opposed his second marriage. Nero seemed unable to manage his lust and his desire for fame. He proceeded to kill his second wife, numerous senators, and others who disagreed with his policies. He believed himself to be a talented singer and lyre player and he performed on stage before the public. The senate deemed his actions to be unseemly for an emperor. Eventually, the senate and the imperial guard turned against Nero, and he had to go into hiding knowing he would be flogged to death if caught. As soldiers surrounded the villa outside Rome where he was staying, Nero committed suicide with the help of two of his aides. He died at the age of thirty-two.

The last persecution ended with a surprise. Begun by Emperor Diocletian in 303 AD, on the advice of his generals, it lasted for ten years. Diocletian himself retired in 305 leaving three generals ruling over different parts of the empire. One of these was Constantine, the only ruler who did not enforce the persecution of Christians within his territory.

By AD 312, war broke out between Constantine and Maxentius, one of the triumvirate of Roman rulers. Reportedly, on the night before the battle, Constantine and his army saw a huge, flaming cross in the evening sky. Emblazoned on the cross were the intertwined letters XP, and the words, "Under this sign you will conquer." Constantine ordered his men to mark their shields with XP, the first letters of Christ's name in Greek. Constantine's army, despite being badly outnumbered, won a major victory the next day over the forces of Maxentius, killing

Maentius in the Battle of Milvian Bridge, and paving the way for Constantine's supreme rule of the Roman Empire.

In the following year, the Edict of Milan proclaimed religious tolerance throughout the lands ruled by Rome. The Edict also mandated the return of property seized in the persecutions. Christians were not only given complete freedom to worship as they pleased, they were also admitted into the ranks of the government and the army.

When Constantine legalized Christianity in AD 313, from ten to thirty percent of the Roman population, depending on which historical estimates are accurate, had already joined the faith. Some of these had avoided persecution by offering incense to pagan gods.

Why did Christianity grow so fast during the almost three hundred years of off and on persecutions? Rodney Stark, in his book, *The Rise of Christianity*, gives three major reasons. The first was the ongoing conversion of the Jews, especially after the complete destruction of Jerusalem in 70 AD. The second reason relates to the status of women and the Church's protection of life. Unlike many Romans, for whom infanticide, particularly of female children was common, Christian women did not practice abortion or infanticide. The birthrate of Christians was therefore much higher. In addition, Christianity raised the status of women so that they held a higher position relative to men than their pagan counterparts

The third reason Stark cites has to do with health care. Two major pestilences devastated the Roman Empire in the three centuries after Christ. The Antonine Plague, which lasted from 161 to 180 AD, struck down people in almost every part of the Empire. A second major plague broke out in 251 AD and remained deadly for at least fifteen years. It killed an estimated thirty to fifty percent of the population of the Roman Empire. Most Roman citizens tried to distance themselves from the afflicted, leaving victims to suffer and die without care or even food and water. Christians, however, at great risk to themselves, provided assistance and tried to nurse plague victims back to health. With care, more victims survived, and those non-Christians who were aided were more likely to embrace the new religion.

In 380 AD, sixty-seven years after Christianity was made legal, Emperor Theodosius made Christianity the official religion of the Roman Empire. The Empire however, continued to grow militarily weaker, and in 476 AD the Roman Empire came to an end. The Germanic peoples who conquered Rome respected much of Roman culture including the Christian religion. For example, Clovis, the first king of the Franks, converted to the Catholic religion of his wife, Clotilde, in 496.

Since the time of Paul and the apostles, Christians missionaries had long been active in spreading the faith. In 250 AD, for example, St. Denis was dispatched from Rome to Paris. In 432, St. Patrick was sent to Ireland and was successful in converting the pagan Irish to Christianity. Perhaps the most influential person of the next century was St. Benedict of Nursia. His Rule for monastic living, written before his death in 547, became the principle way of life for monks to the present day. Beginning in the sixth century, hundreds of monasteries following the Rule of St. Benedict were built all over Europe.

Monasteries were centers of spirituality, and monks took vows of poverty, chastity and obedience. Each religious community was completely self sustaining, with a farm, a corral for animals, vineyard, bakery, kitchen, chapel and small rooms for the residents. Monasteries also provided accommodations for travelers and care for the sick. The monks laboriously copied by hand the classical books of Greece and Rome.

Besides their spiritual mandate, the monasteries were instrumental in preserving the knowledge handed down from Greece and Rome. In total absence of the printing press, which was to come much later, they spent vast amounts of time copying by hand not only the spiritual works of the church fathers, but also the secular works of antiquity. The monasteries served not only as the world's only bookmakers of the time, but also provided the only schooling available. The small monastery schools supplied education not only for priests and monks but also for nobles and even orphans who were taken in and cared for. Not until the ninth century did Carlemagne decree that the major churches, the cathedrals, should also establish schools open to the general public. Unfortunately, the value of women receiving educational opportunity was not recognized until much later in history.

Although there were many kingdoms in the early middle ages, there were as yet no nation states. Almost all education was conducted in monasteries or in the cathedral schools. Such an education was imbued with Christian doctrine and belief, and in time, all Europe became an almost totally Christian domain.

The heritage received and passed on from the Romans included many literary works, but surprisingly, very little scientific knowledge. The Romans were great architects, builders, and sanitary engineers, but they were not given to scientific analysis.

As a result, most unexplainable events during the middle ages were seen to be the work of God, angels or demons. Belief in miracles was common and accepted with faith.

The mind set of the medieval man or woman, especially in the early middle ages, was religious. God and the angels and saints were visualized as being close, and heaven was directly above the earth. God could look down and see his creation.

With the beginning of towns and the relative prosperity of the eleventh and twelfth centuries, the citizens began to build beautiful churches. Most people still lived in one or two room houses, but they took pride in their church and were willing to donate years of labor to the cause of creating a beautiful structure that would represent their town.

The strong religious feelings of the early middle ages continued into fourteenth and fifteenth centuries giving impetus for the wealth of masterful religious paintings of the Renaissance. There was a striking difference in art, however, because for the first time since the Roman period, representations took on the likeness of the people themselves. The majority of Renaissance paintings remain religious, but they capture the likenesses of real people in an extraordinary way never before accomplished. The Renaissance celebrated not only God, but man. The beautiful paintings of the virgin and child are for the most part Italian women whose images still grace the walls of great museums throughout the world.

With the waning of the Renaissance in the sixteenth century, major changes were developing which would shake the religious world view of many. The first of these was the Reformation. Luther's challenge to the Roman Church was the first of a number of reformers who established other forms of Protestantism (protest) against what had been the "Universal Church."

Certainly the Roman Church had its faults—the excessive selling of indulgences for huge sums being only one. As a human institution, it had its share of miscreant priests and even high placed church officials. Subsequent major church councils later in the century dealt with the abuses, but it was too late. The unity of Christendom under one faith was shattered.

Another vital change was ushered in by the growth of technology. With the publishing of the book by Copernicus in 1543, *On the revolutions Of The Celestial Spheres*, suddenly the view that God and heaven was directly overhead was placed in doubt. Copernicus showed that earth revolves around the sun, and not vice versa as Christians had always believed. Proof came later when Galileo trained his telescope on the "wandering stars" and found they were actually planets, like earth but different.

The church reacted, sentencing Galileo to prison, which was reduced to house arrest. Suddenly, science had taken away the old certainty of most people that God was right overhead, looking after His creation.

The majority of people, however, had little understanding of the new discoveries and lived their lives with faith as they always had. It was the educated who realized the significance of the new ideas. In time, more discoveries followed, which particularly in the nineteenth and twentieth centuries, resulted in numerous inventions that began to affect the lives of ordinary people.

It was in the twentieth century that life changed dramatically. The automobile, electricity, the radio, refrigerators, air conditioning, indoor plumbing, telephones and computers became the everyday stuff of life. At the same time, in both the United States and Europe, a high school education became the norm rather than the limited primary education afforded people in the nineteenth century. With high school, students learned in science classes about the solar system, the stars, and about chemistry and biology. In many classrooms they also studied Darwin's theory of evolution. In 1962 the United States Supreme Court banned prayer and the reading of the bible in public schools. Students could learn about science, but they could no longer learn about God. Perhaps not surprisingly, the April 16th, 1966 cover of Time Magazine asked, in full page lettering, "Is God Dead?

The coming of the modern era

Many are unaware of the major transformation of human life that has occurred in a relatively short period of time. Not only our lifestyle, but also our way of thinking has been impacted by change.

Imagine for a moment what it was like to live in the time of our great grandparents. Let us quickly review how much our lives have changed in the past one hundred years. Then we will consider if these technological and cultural changes have altered our way of thinking.

Many of the inventions or discoveries of the eighteen hundreds didn't become standard in American and European homes until the twentieth century. When they did become common, they drastically modified our way of life.

Think for a moment what life must have been like at the turn of the century. In 1900, most Americans didn't have running water, indoor toilets, radio or television, a car or even electricity. There were no refrigerators to keep food fresh, though in the cities some had ice boxes, kept cool by a large block of ice delivered as needed by the iceman with his horse drawn carriage. Baths, if taken at all, were usually a Saturday night affair. Water, which had to be drawn from a pump or well, was heated on a wood or charcoal stove and poured into a large washtub or freestanding bathtub placed at a convenient place on the floor. Adults went first, followed by children and then the baby—all using the same water.

Going to the outhouse to relieve oneself was an uncomfortable chore. On bitter, cold days, one didn't take long, as there was no heat and freezing of exposed skin was a distinct possibility. In warm weather, outhouses were terribly smelly and a gathering place for flies, mosquitoes and spiders.

Lighting was poor. The smoky glow of kerosene lamps was usually the only illumination available after the sun went down. People were not connected to each other in the sense we use connected today. There was no mass media other than newspapers and a few magazines. Even radio, invented in 1895, did not become readily available until the nineteen twenties and thirties when electricity finally reached most American towns. Those on the farm had to wait many more years before they were "electrified." When telephones became common in the 40's, people could at last reach someone they cared about without having to make a trip. What a different life our great great grandparents experienced.

Today we are connected in many ways. Our personal phones, computers, television, radio, iPods, iPads, Skype, etc., enable us to connect with whoever we want almost anytime we want. Our life style of comfort and convenience is far better than that of even kings and queens of an earlier age. In fact, we are like royalty, able to make a variety of personal choices that those who came before us scarcely dreamed of. In earlier times, we needed to interact closely with those we lived with, with people in our town, those at our church, and at our schools. We needed to connect with them because we had no other contacts. Life then was lived moment by moment with family members and with neighbors. In the absence of welfare, unemployment compensation, nursing homes and social security, people depended on each other to get by in times of need.

In the early part of the 1900's, life was not easy. However, in some ways it was much simpler. Today, with all the labor saving appliances and all our communication systems that are powered by electricity, life is physically easier, but in some ways much more complicated. We have entered a new era.

Living in the present—the Twenty-First Century

What impact does substantially more comfort and independence have on our lives? Today we choose what to wear, what to drive, what to watch on TV, who to associate with, and even what to believe. All these aspects of our lives are left to our personal discretion. We have freedom to do as we like, and most of us enjoy making the most of our freedom.

With so many choices, it is often hard for young people to make decisions affecting their future. What kind of work to do, whom to marry, what to believe, what type of career, and on what to focus their energies? These life choices are far harder than in the past when fewer options were available.

Ultimately, I suspect, many try to get by by not making choices at all. Or, by making some choices and not others. It may be easy for a son or daughter whose father owns or is employed at a thriving business to join the firm. The vast majority of young adults, however, usually find it far more trying to settle into satisfactory and gainful employment. However, it is quite easy in this age of tolerance for an unmarried man and woman to live together. No commitment is necessary. No permanent choice is required.

There are many reasons why it is more difficult in the modern age to make decisions. Surprisingly, a major cause is television—particularly TV advertising. People say they pay no attention to advertising. Nevertheless, ads do affect us. Why else would companies spend hundreds of thousands of dollars for air time? We will consider the extraordinary impact of television in an upcoming chapter.

Of course, the tube is only one of the media vying for our attention. Cell phones, the internet, Email, newspapers, magazines and billboards all reach out to us. Is it any wonder that people become distracted? So much is coming at us from so many sources it can be difficult to think. Nevertheless, we do a good job of remembering things of importance. Particularly numbers. We know our social security number, our address, birth dates, telephone numbers, password numbers, combination lock numbers, etc. We may find it hard to understand how ancient peoples

remembered the words to verses before they were finally written down. Those people would likely find it just as amazing how we can keep so many unrelated numbers in our heads.

In the days before radio, television and phones, quiet times were frequent. Today, a substantial percentage of people feel uncomfortable with silence. Whether at home, in the car or taking a walk, they always have either the TV, radio, or music playing, or they talk on the phone. Many students feel they cannot study unless they are at the same time tuned in. They need to hear something to be able to concentrate.

In just one hundred years, the majority of Americans and most Europeans have gone from practically no media to almost constant media access. From no radio, no television, no computer, no phone and no car to today's media blitz. One hundred years is a very short time in the history of civilization. How does the constant presence of communication media affect us? In particular, how does it affect our psyche. We know our lives have been changed by technology. Has this same technology changed the way we think? If so, how?

Five concepts that changed Western thought

Most people agree that the way North Americans and Europeans think is not the same as Orientals. There is also a vast difference between Chinese, Indian, Bolivian and Arabian thought. On the other hand, much of the Western World, including Europe and Russia, tend to think the same way. Not that they are in agreement on any particular topic. It is the *way* the West thinks that tends to be quite similar.

The reason lies in our common background. Our heritage of Greek and Roman thought and the influence of the Renaissance and the Age of Reason permeates our thinking. More recently, America and the West have been strongly influenced by other ways of looking at the world and its people.

Ideas that changed the way we think

The Renaissance brought major changes in thought, art, and culture to Europe and eventually to the Americas. Prior to the Fifteenth Century, the Roman Church was the main arbiter of art, fashion, learning and religion. Artistic expression during the Middle Ages was stylized and ethereal, and its main purpose was to teach and to arouse a feeling of devotion. The Renaissance broke with the focus on religious concepts and began to celebrate the beauty of the here and now. Inspired by a renewal of Greek and Roman art and letters, Italians led the world not only in realistic painting, but also in attempts to solve some of the major human problems of the day.

The focus on seeing the world as composed of matter and making improvements is part of the mind-set of people of the Western World. This way of looking at things has led to inventions that make life more comfortable as well as to weapons of war that have ended the lives of millions. This mind-set has also led to many philosophies and the formulation of psychologies that try to make sense of the human condition and the social order. It is noteworthy that most major psychological and philosophical theories depart from the religious world view of Christianity, as well as other religious perspectives. Was something missing in the Christian world view?

Apparently many have thought so, for during and after the Renaissance a great many different philosophies were conceived and debated. Whether Marxism, socialism, Freudian psychology, naturalism, or many other philosophies, almost all attempt to explain the world and human nature without reference to God.

We moderns have internalized at least some aspects of these modern isms, often without realizing it. Leaving aside political ideologies, let's take a look at some of the points of view currently in vogue in our culture. Do they have personal meaning for us?

The following is a short list of ideologies prevalent in American and European culture. Given first is the name, followed by a short definition. Beneath the definition are two spaces where you and perhaps a friend can record your own personal agreement or disagreement with the ideology. Use **0** for no agreement, **1** for some agreement, **2** for moderate agreement, and **3** for substantially in agreement with the ism. When finished, total your number.

Hedonism

The belief that pleasure is the highest good in life. A hedonist strives to maximize his or her pleasure and minimize pain. Pleasure is often thought of as the pleasure of sex and of good food, but some hedonists emphasize pleasures of the mind. In their quest for pleasure, hedonists do not ordinarily subscribe to a moral code or religious ideology that might put limits on their pursuit of pleasure.

_____|_____

Social Darwinism

The belief that people in society compete for survival and that superior individuals, social groups, and races become more powerful and wealthy. Social Darwinists assert that those best able to survive demonstrate their fitness by accumulating property, wealth, and social status. Poverty, according to the theory, proves an individual or group's unfitness. Often, those who subscribe to the beliefs of Social Darwinism will not come to the aid of those in need because to do so is against their world outlook that they should prevail over the weak.

————————|————————

Materialism

Is a belief that everything is material, or a state of matter. People who hold materialistic viewpoints believe that the laws of science are able to explain everything that happens. Things that cannot be seen or measured by science do not exist. Soul, spirit, and mind do not exist, and the working of the human mind is only chemical/electrical events occurring in the brain. People, despite their native aptitudes and learned abilities, are only animals having no soul or spiritual dimension. Life here and now is all that is important. Present well-being and material possessions are the measure of success. Strict materialists have no religious beliefs. They do not accept the idea of heaven or hell. They live only in the present world.

————————|————————

Nihilism

Is a philosophy that believes that life is without objective meaning, purpose or intrinsic value. As such, it opposes traditional values, beliefs and authority. Postmodernism, a newer trend, is related to nihilism in that it questions the certainty of scientific, or objective efforts to describe reality. Postmodernists tend to be highly skeptical of religious and philosophical truths that claim to be valid for all peoples. Since postmodernists deny the existence of any ultimate principles, they hold that truths or beliefs are only relative to a person, a group, a culture, or a nation, but certainly not for everyone.

———————⌐———————

Deism

Deism is listed here because it is a semi-religious philosophy that maintains that reason, not revelation, is the best guide for understanding God and the universe. Deists believe that a powerful being or entity was necessary in order for the universe to be created. They maintain that the laws of motion, gravity, etc. permit the universe to continue on its course unaided, without intervention. Most Deists therefore reject miracles, prophecy, the bible and organized religion as being unnecessary and corrupting the simplicity of the natural order. Deists believe that a supreme being set the universe in motion, but they do not believe that "he" is active in creation. Some Deists believe in life after death, others do not.

———————⌐———————

After adding up the numbers, how did you score? Three or less and you're probably not much affected by these isms, which for the most part run counter to Christian values. More than seven points most likely indicates your acceptance of at least some of the currently popular ideologies.

This short list of major philosophical perspectives is certainly not all-inclusive, but it does illustrate major ideas currently in vogue. These philosophies or world views can be compared with the basic beliefs of the four major world religions—Christianity, Islam, Hinduism, and Buddhism.

Religious world views

Christianity:

By most ranking methods, Christianity is the largest religion, with approximately two billion adherents. The followers of this religion call themselves Christians. They believe that Jesus Christ is the Son of God, the Messiah who was prophesied in the Old Testament, the book of scripture Christians have in common with Judaism. Most Christians believe Jesus entered our world born of a virgin for the purpose of making known our relationship with God. Through his ministry and teachings he shows how to lead a virtuous life. His subsequent suffering and death on a cross is seen as the price paid for the redemption of the sins of man. Though now in heaven, he remains vitally interested in men and women. Most denominations teach that Christ will return to judge the living and the dead, raising up those who have led satisfactory lives to eternal life with him in heaven.

The majority of Christians also believe Christ founded his church before he died and named one of his apostles, Peter, to be its head. The church Christ founded was persecuted by the Jews and by the Romans but eventually became the main religion of Europe. From there it spread to much of the world through missionary work especially during the Age of Exploration. During the Reformation in the 1500's, various major branches of Christianity arose which have continued to the present day. Almost all these versions of Christianity are guided by the Bible and especially the New Testament, which records Christ's works and teachings during his short life on earth.

Islam:

Islam is the second largest religion in the world with approximately one and a half billion adherents. Muslims believe in one God—Allah, and trace their faith back to the great prophets—Abraham, David, Moses and Jesus. The last prophet, Muhammad, in 622 AD clarified and purified the faith and added to the New and Old Testament the sacred texts of the Koran and the Hadith. The Koran contains the words of Allah, "the One True God," and the Hadith is a collection of Muhammad's sayings.

Muslims do not believe in the Trinity or in the divinity of Christ, nor that he died on a cross for sins. Like Christians, they believe in paradise, Satan and hell. Muslims who sincerely repent and submit to Allah will go to paradise after death.

The duties of all Muslims include reciting the Shahadah at least once, praying five times a day while facing toward the Kaaba, donating to charity at the 2.5% minimum charity tax, fasting during the month of Ramadan, and if physically able, making a pilgrimage to Mecca at least once during their lifetime. Muslims are also to avoid gambling, alcohol and drugs.

Hinduism:

Is the third largest religion, numbering approximately nine hundred million adherents. Unlike Christianity, Judaism and Islam, the Bible contributes nothing to its doctrines. In fact, early Hinduism precedes the Bible. Hinduism is the main religion of India and had its beginning sometime after 4000 BC. Hindus believe that everything is incorporated into the oneness of Brahman. Life's purpose is to realize that we are part of the totality of Brahman and to understand the unity of all existence. This understanding is reached by going through cycles of birth, life and death. Karma—the sum of a person's good and bad deeds, determines his or her next reincarnation which can be lower, in the form of an insect or animal, or higher, in the form of a person with discernment and devotion to Brahman.

Most Hindus adhere to a strict caste system, which determines their standing in society. They are born into a higher or lower caste depending on the karma of their previous life. Good deeds and selfless acts and thoughts help to raise one to a higher level in the next reincarnation. The ultimate goal of Hindus is to end the cycles of reincarnation by becoming one with Brahman.

Buddhism:

Has developed from the precepts of Siddhartha Gautama, who after many years of searching, reached enlightenment and began his teachings in 535 B.C. Assuming the title of Buddha, Siddhartha promoted the "The Middle Way" as the path to enlightenment instead of self aggrandizement or hedonism. Buddhism has spread throughout Asia and currently has approximately 350 million adherents.

Buddhists believe that suffering is part of life on earth. However, through detachment from desire and self-ego, one can rise above afflictions. Ultimately, through meditation, kindness in word and deed, and successive reincarnations, Nirvana can be reached. Nirvana is a state where there is no pain, no desire and an end to the individual self.

As of 2010, these four religions have the largest number of adherents. Judaism is currently the religion of less than one percent of the world's peoples, according to the World Christian Data base. However the Jewish religion provides a foundation for the two most populous faiths, Christianity and Islam.

The four major faiths have different views of heaven. Christians, for the most part, see heaven as an intimate closeness with the Lord along with an end to all pain and suffering. Christians expect to experience what has long been called "The Beatific Vision." Beatific is a Latin word meaning "making happy," and Christianity emphasizes that those in heaven will have an intimate knowledge of God which will bring them eternal happiness. The Old Testament gives some information on what heaven will be like. The New Testament has many more references to the afterlife, making it clear that man will not be an inanimate spirit. Man's perfected, resurrected body will join his spirit in heaven.

The Muslim view of heaven is much more descriptive and physical. Like the Christian view, there will be no pain or suffering. There will be complete happiness as well as the sight of God—Allah. However, the Koran further describes cool shade and breezes, rivers of water, wine, milk and honey, luscious foods, and beautiful furnishings and clothing, etc. In addition, lovely virginal companions with beautiful lustrous eyes are afforded to males. Women, however, will have only one husband, ordinarily their earthly spouses.

The Hindu and Buddhist view of reaching eternal life may be hard for Westerners to understand. Both Hindus and Buddhists look forward to reaching a plane of existence where there is no pain. For Hindus, there is oneness with Brahman, and for Buddhists, reaching the state of Nirvana, a blissful state of knowing removed from all desires and passions.

Has Christianity changed our way of life?

If Christ had not come, would we be living in a different world? Christianity arose and developed during the age of the Roman Empire. To an extent, it was limited by the culture of the time. However, it soon deviated from Roman culture especially after Christianity became legal in 313 AD. Taking a look at four specific changes Christ's followers made to Roman culture, we can decide if they remain part of our culture today.

Care of the sick.

The Romans carried on and sometimes improved on the medical knowledge and practice of the Greeks. They knew how to set broken bones, and they used the pain killing drugs of opium, henbane and mandrake. They were even able to surgically repair hernias and minimize cataracts. However, they had little success fighting diseases.

The Romans learned much about caring for wounds as the result of their many battles, and they even provided care facilities or "hospitals" for military personnel. They had treatment centers for gladiators, the best of whom, like today's football players, were valuable to their owners. However, there was no hospital for the ordinary Roman citizen. Even those who could afford doctors were treated and cared for in their own home.

Shortly after the end of the persecutions, Christians acted to provide basic health care for all. The Church Council of Nicaea in 325 directed the bishops to establish a hospice in every city that had a cathedral. Those first care facilities were also directed to provide temporary shelter for the poor and lodging for Christian pilgrims.

The first "real" hospital, with adjacent houses for nurses and doctors, was built by St. Basil in AD 369. More hospitals continued to be built in the years that followed, and sick bay areas became a common feature of monasteries, which, by the sixth century had become numerous everywhere—in Italy, Spain, France, North Africa, Ireland and Britain. During the Middle Ages, health care continued to be the province of orders of monks and nuns. The religious nature of health care continued in Europe and then in America until quite recent times. Even today, many hospitals retain the names of saints and reflect their founding or operation by religious orders.

Education

The role of Christianity in preserving and dispersing knowledge is well known. In particular, the care taken to make copies of the books of Greek and Roman antiquity has left us with a record of the philosophical, literary and practical works of the ages. Monks worked tirelessly copying ancient manuscripts. They searched the then-known world to find surviving works to add to their collections. They carefully made additional copies and lent books to monasteries in other countries so that the wealth of knowledge would not be lost.

Many monks were well educated, and people living near monasteries could avail themselves of the monastic schools. Parents frequently sent their male children to be cared for and educated at the monastery. Homeless orphans were taken in, fed, clothed, educated and taught an occupation. Those who were able to master demanding studies often became monks or priests. In particular, the children of nobles received an education at these schools.

In the ninth century, Charlemagne, by decree and by his active interest, substantially increased the number of schools providing education not only for the noble class but also for peasants. Charlemagne recognized that priests and monks were the main literate class, and he directed the monasteries and the cathedrals to either open schools or to increase the size of their schools so more could attend.

In time, some of the cathedral schools expanded in size and courses offered and became major centers of learning. Some well known universities that were formerly cathedral schools include the University of Paris, the University of Bologna, Oxford and the University of Cambridge. Though most of the teachers during the Middle

Ages were priests and monks, the curriculum was expanded to include subjects that were important for men of affairs, that is, nobles, merchants and accountants. Unfortunately, during the eleventh and twelfth Centuries, women were still not admitted to most schools, though some did receive instruction at home from private tutors.

Throughout the Middle Ages and until modern times, church schools have been the norm. Thomas Jefferson believed public education should be available for all children. As early as 1785, he lobbied the Virginia General Assembly in these words: "Every child is entitled to three years of instruction in reading, writing and arithmetic." His ideas were not taken up until much later. In the meantime, private schools and charitable and religious institutions provided for most children the only education available. In the years following the Civil War, more states began providing free education so that by 1900 a public education up to elementary school level was accessible to almost all children in the United States.

Science

It may be surprising to many that Christianity has fostered science. Has the comfortable life we live today come about because of Christ? How can that be? Certainly, Jesus didn't focus on material things. Didn't he say, "My kingdom is not of this world?" Nevertheless, the case can easily be made that because of Christianity we have television, airplanes, cell phones, miracle drugs, and automobiles, etc.

In no other culture, be it Egyptian, Greek, Roman, or Muslim has the drive for technological improvements been so strong. For the Greeks and Romans, labor saving devices were not important—they had slaves to do the hard or dirty work. Furthermore, their pantheistic religious beliefs obscured the inherent orderliness of the universe. They didn't clearly recognize that nature had laws, and that those laws could be harnessed to benefit mankind.

Often unrecognized, is the Islamic contribution to scientific endeavor. During the Golden Age of Islam, from 750 AD to 1259 AD, the Muslim world extended from Spain to the Middle East and into India. It was the most advanced culture in the world. From China they learned to make paper, from India they refined and developed the system of numbers we use today. Their understanding of the workings of the human body and the development of pharmacology was unsurpassed in the West for hundreds of years. Their prolific translations of Greek and Roman manuscripts, using paper—far cheaper than animal hide, afforded the transmission of ideas to a much wider audience and likely helped to usher in the Renaissance.

The belief that a good and reasonable God made the universe is shared by Jews, Christians and Muslims. This conviction has allowed men and women of science to assume that creation is orderly, with discoverable laws and principles. From the inception of the earliest monastery classroom before the fall of Rome, to the cathedral schools and the rise of universities, the Church has fostered learning and logical thinking. Almost all of the major men of science from the fifteenth through the nineteenth century were Christian, either Catholic or Protestant. Most of them learned in schools taught by religious educators or founded by religious orders. Men like Johannes Gutenberg, inventor of the printing press, Nicolaus Copernicus, who discovered that the earth goes around the sun, Galileo, who first saw the planets with his telescope, Michael Faraday, the inventor of the electric motor and even the Wright Brothers, who built the first successful airplane, were strongly influenced by religion.

Without education, fostered through the ages by Christianity, it is unlikely that science would have developed in the Western World or during Islam's Golden Age. Instead, civilization would likely be in a primitive state like it still is in many third world countries which until recently did not know the liberating influence of Christianity.

Did Christianity Civilize Society?

Whether Christianity contributed to making society better and less callous may still be open to question. As we have noted, Christianity developed within the Roman Empire, an age we would consider today to be a time of unusual contrasts. On the one hand, the Romans achieved unrivaled accomplishments in construction, sanitation, and military prowess. They also assimilated the arts and letters of Greece and made contributions of their own. On the other hand, the ancient Romans are known for their extreme cruelty and bloodlust.

The Roman emperors did not invent crucifixion, but they used it regularly against peoples who rose up against Roman rule, as well as on criminals and slaves. The parents of Christ—Mary and Joseph, would have known its horror firsthand. Four miles from Nazareth, 2000 Jewish freedom fighters were crucified in 4 BC. Crucifixion is an especially agonizing and slow death. Victims suffer for hours or days while being exposed to weather, insects, birds and animals.

The Romans seemed to enjoy inflicting pain and suffering. Unfortunately, for followers of Christ, their increasing numbers in the Empire eventually brought them recognition. When Christians refused to offer incense to the Roman Gods, they were tortured and executed in ways we would today consider today to be extremely cruel and unusual. Besides crucifixion, Romans employed burning at the stake, the rack, grilling alive and many other methods to torture and dispatch victims. Tens of thousands, perhaps hundreds of thousands of people (records were not kept) died in vile and sadistic ways.

Strange as it may seem, death was the main form of entertainment in the Roman Empire. Thousands attended the frequent shows in the amphitheaters. The largest arena is the still standing Coliseum in Rome which held over 50,000 spectators. It is estimated a million people met death over its hundreds of years of history. Most died in gladiatorial combat, the event most favored by the spectators.

Two hundred and thirty of these Roman arenas have been found as far away as England, Algeria, The Netherlands, Scotland, Israel, Turkey and Romania. Unlike the theaters, which were semicircular structures used for plays and various shows, the arenas were built like football stadiums—enclosed on all sides. There was no escape for gladiators, slaves or Christians sentenced to die by hungry, ferocious animals or the sword. As time went on, the taste of the crowds called for ever more bloodthirsty battles and deaths. On some days, as many as a thousand gladiators, criminals and slaves died on the sands of the arenas.

The bishops, who often had to go into hiding, exhorted Christians not to attend the obscene dramas of the stage or the bloody battles of the arenas. However, until Christianity was legalized, there was nothing they could do to change the entertainment preferences of the Roman leaders and people. In 325 AD, Constantine, the first Christian emperor, banned the gladiator games. Unfortunately, his edict did not completely end the battles, though after this date they gradually declined in size and number of spectators. It proved difficult to completely end a form of entertainment that had existed for hundreds of years.

Though the Roman Empire officially ended in 476 AD, Christianity continued its amazing growth. The majority of the invading peoples coming into Italy, Spain, France and Germany and beyond eventually accepted Christianity and its values. Public execution by the torture of crucifixion was outlawed. Torture did not end completely, but for the most part it was done in private—often in dungeons away from public view and the knowledge of the church.

With the complete breakdown of the Empire, most of Europe dissolved into major and minor kingdoms and the feudal system. Poor farming people needed protection and aligned themselves with major landowners who built fortresses and tried to keep enemies at bay by means of retained soldiers. In time, these men became knights.

For the most part, clerics were the only people who could read and write. Because of this and their control of religious belief, they a had marked influence on society during the middle ages. Every manor and court, no matter how small, needed someone who could keep track of accounts, who could read and write treaties, and who could administer the sacraments of religion.

There is little doubt that clerics were responsible for the development of the code of chivalry. Knights were the soldiers and policemen of the time with superior weaponry and training. The church tried to bind them to a code of honor so that they would not use their power to violate the rights of others. By the time of Charlemagne, and probably before, the ideas of serving the liege lord, protecting the weak and defenseless, keeping the faith, to respecting the honor of women, obeying those in authority and never turning one's back on a foe, etc. had probably become a tradition. Not that living with honor and glory was always the norm, but it was the ideal that was more or less expected of the fighting class. Later in the middle ages, those who would be knights were required to bathe, fast, spend much time in prayer and formally be dubbed a knight in a more or less grand ceremony.

For a time, the Church was even successful in limiting the waging of war. The formal Pax Dei, or Peace of God, was first instituted late in the tenth century at the Synod of Charroux. It formalized injunctions against injuring peasants, women and clerics, and its message gradually spread throughout Europe. The code was enacted with great display by having knights swear on the relics of saints before a crowd of peasants, priests, monks and even bishops. The Truce of God, a separate rule, limited the prosecution of war to certain days of the week. The penalty for infractions of these rules was usually excommunication and stiff fines.

Gradually, however, the increasing power of kings and the rise of national states during the thirteenth century led to a decline in church influence on the conduct of war.

Killing for God?

The Inquisition

In the many centuries since the fall of Rome, blood has continued to be shed, most of it in times of war. However, the church is itself implicated in its initiation of the Inquisition. How could an institution that had done so much to end cruel and unusual punishment promulgate it?

The Inquisition began in Southern France early in the Thirteenth Century as a means of subduing the Cathars, a sect believing that all matter is evil, that having children is wrong, and a sect which rejected the sacraments and Christ's resurrection. The Spanish inquisition which followed was much larger in scale. It was also more cruel because it was started and run by the Spanish government. Begun in 1478, it was active mainly in the first one hundred and fifty years of its history, though the last official victim was executed in 1826.

Those who separated from the Catholic Church during and after the Reformation wildly overestimated the total number of Inquisition deaths. More recent scholarship since 1965 has been conducted by a number of historians who systematically looked at court records. These records show that the total number of people killed is somewhere between 3000 and 6000. This number represents approximately two percent of those tried in both the religious and secular tribunals. While a small number compared to the vast numbers who died in the internecine wars of Europe, it remains a discredit to the Roman Church.

The Crusades

There is no doubt that the Church promulgated the Crusades. The question of whether the crusades were justified is still debated. In one important sense they were.

For centuries Rome and then Constantinople battled the Persians. In the seventh century an even more powerful adversary arose from the western highlands of Arabia. They were the Muslims, who in holy wars of conquest defeated the Persians, wrested control of the Holy Land, defeated Egypt and North Africa, and by 715 AD had conquered Spain.

In 717 AD, the Muslims launched a major offensive against Constantinople itself. With an armada of almost 2000 ships and 160,000 fighting men, they sought to surround and starve into submission the then most populous city in the world.

Leo III, a successful general who had recently seized the throne was prepared. He had stockpiled food and strengthened the walls of the city. He had also prepared great quantities of "Greek fire" a still secret substance that caused enemy ships to burst into flame. After a 12 month siege of Constantinople, and the loss of most of their ships and manpower, the Muslims went home defeated. Constantinople's success in beating back the Muslims protected Eastern Europe from Muslim invasions for hundreds of years.

In the west, from Spain the Muslims pressed into present day France where they seized the cities of Narbonne, Avignon, Carcassonne, and Nimes. They lost a major battle at Toulouse, in 721 AD, when they were surrounded by a large force as they were laying siege to the city. Nevertheless, in 731 they extended their dominion in southern France and won a major battle at the Garonne River. Proceeding deeper into France toward Paris via Tours, they were met by the army of Charles Martel, the leader of the Franks.

Having seized higher ground, Charles played a waiting game, aligning his force of approximately 15,000 to 30,000 mostly foot soldiers with long spears in difficult to penetrate phalanxes. The Muslims, mounted on horses and with superior numbers, tried numerous times to break the rock hard defense. After several days of waiting they charged up the hill and were hacked to death by the broad swords of the French. Their general was killed in the battle, and their remaining forces retreated in the night back to Spain.

Most historians believe that this major defeat and subsequent battles won by Charles were instrumental in saving Europe not only from Muslim domination but also kept Christianity rather than Islam as the major religion of the western world.

Despite beating back the Islamic jihad, most eighth century Europeans were not united and were instead ruled by lords or kings of small principalities. The ability to finance sizeable armies was quite limited and the lack of shipping for troop transport prevented Europeans from attacking Muslim forces across the sea. Even the very gradual reconquest of Spain took hundreds of years and was not fully completed until 1492.

Nevertheless, by 1000 AD, with rising prosperity and the formation of larger kingdoms, Europeans finally had sufficient strength to fight a foreign war.

The first opportunity came in response to the takeover of the Holy Land by the Seljuk Turks after the Battle of Manzikert in 1071 AD. Prior to this time Palestine was controlled by the Fatimid Caliphate, who allowed Christian pilgrims access to the holy sites of Jerusalem.

The Seljuk Turks were not nearly as tolerant of pilgrims, and reports of their mistreatment got back to Europe. In 1095, the Emperor of Constantinople, Alexios I, sent envoys to Pope Urban II asking for help in defeating the Turks.

In Western Europe religious fervor was high and Pope Urban's appeal to return the Holy Land to Christian ownership met with strong acceptance. However, while the Europeans were ready to risk their lives for the cause, they appeared to have little knowledge of logistics or military preparedness. The flight distance from Paris to Jerusalem is over 2000 miles and, of course, the walking distance is much greater and required crossing the usually snow-covered Alps. Consequently most crusaders never reached Jerusalem and vast numbers died along the way of sickness, bitter weather and skirmishes for which they were unprepared. Others were taken prisoner and sold into slavery. This was particularly true of the children who marched in the Children's Crusade.

Some crusaders had enough money to afford ship transportation, though they were likely in the minority. A tragic outcome of many of the Crusades was the indiscriminate killing of Jews along the way. The medieval mentality blamed Jews for the crucifixion of Christ. This violence was never condoned by the popes, and in fact the clergy tried to stop the slaughters, usually to no avail.

Given the general lack of organization and the long distance, it is surprising that any of the crusades were militarily successful. The first crusade did wrest control of Jerusalem and several important cities from the Muslims in 1098 and 1099. A Latin Kingdom was established in the Middle East which allowed pilgrims to travel in safety overland to Jerusalem. Less than 100 years later, Saladin, the sultan of Egypt and Syria, recaptured Jerusalem and held it despite the successes of Richard the Lionheart in the third crusade.

The only other crusade that had any success in retaking Jerusalem was the sixth, led by Emperor Frederick II. Through his negotiations, not battle, he managed to gain control of Jerusalem in 1228. The agreement lasted sixteen years until the city came under siege and was completely razed in 1244.

Otherwise, the crusades were military failures and caused the loss of at least hundreds of thousands if not millions of lives, especially on the Christian side.

Witch Trials

The burning or hanging of witches is another sad chapter in history. The first major witch trials started in present day Switzerland and nearby France in civil courts between 1427 and 1447. In Valais, Switzerland, approximately 100 accused witches were executed in a mass burning.

The height of the witch trials in Europe came later, in the hundred and fifty years between 1550 and 1700 in the countries of Switzerland, Germany, and Eastern France. Significantly, it developed in regions of Europe considerably affected by the Reformation, where rival sects of Christianity sought to impose their own brand of religion on each other. The strongly Catholic countries of Italy and Spain had few witch hunts, and the Inquisition itself almost always pardoned any witch who confessed and repented.

The total number of witches who were condemned to death was highly exaggerated until twentieth century scholarship and scrutiny of court records brought to light that not millions, but somewhere between 30,000 and 60,000 witches were sentenced to death. In the American colonies, approximately 40 died, including 20 in the infamous Salem Witch Trials.

Twentieth Century Genocide

The worst death tolls were to come in the Twentieth Century and had very little to do with religion. In both Russia and Germany, dictators managed to take control of Christian countries. Hitler was politically astute enough not to alienate the population of Germany, which at the time was composed of approximately two thirds Protestant and one third Catholic denominations. In fact, in making public statements, he at times sounded as if he believed in God. His real ideology was based on Social Darwinism and the creation of an Aryan master race. To that end, he sterilized mixed race Germans, liquidated handicapped and retarded people, and gassed the "inferior" races of Jews, Gypsies and Poles. Hitler and his henchmen killed approximately six million people.

Joseph Stalin, the dictator who rose to power in Communist Russia, is held by many historians to be responsible for the deaths of more people than Hitler. Not only did he close the Russian Orthodox churches and execute the clergy, he also orchestrated numerous purges killing more than a million people whom he suspected of real or imagined threats to his strong man rule. According to official Soviet records, 14 million people were sent to the gulag prison camps during Stalin's reign—many of them dying there due to lack of food and harsh conditions. Seven or eight million more were deported to remote areas of the

Soviet Union where as many as half of them died from the extreme cold or starvation. Incredulously, Stalin is believed to have killed more Russians than the people of Russia's military enemies, starving millions in the Ukraine and sending millions more to be worked to death in labor camps. Stalin, like Karl Marx, had no use for religion, believing that religion was the opiate of the people.

.

Is TV influencing our beliefs?

Television is a very recent development in comparison to the many thousands of years of human history. Nevertheless, TV screens are everywhere in Western nations, and are fast appearing in third world countries. Does television influence our beliefs? In particular, are we influenced by watching a great deal of television? Recent Nielsen statistics show that Americans watch almost five hours of television a day.

According to a 2010 Kaiser Family Foundation study, youth ages 8 to 18 devote an average of 7 hours and 38 minutes using entertainment media in a typical day. This is not only television, but includes multi-media cell phones, iPods and video games. With so much time spent being tuned in, it may be no surprise to learn that the majority of youth do not regularly attend church services.

Most people are aware that even prime time TV is rife with violence, sexual content and profanity. It is estimated that the average American teen will see 200,000 acts of violence by the time he or she reaches 18. Even MTV, originally a music channel, regularly features musical videos depicting sex and violence. Unfortunately, it is mostly youth, teenagers and young adults who watch the show. It is also primarily young people who enjoy playing addictive and often quite bloody video games.

The focus on violence, whether in newscasts or in programming, has two major effects. One, it increases the likelihood that people, especially youth, will commit violent crimes, and two, it promotes fear in both young and old. Increasingly, due to the real and simulated violence seen on TV, the world and even the immediate neighborhood can be seen as dangerous. The result is less casual friendliness, a fear of talking to strangers, and a heightened dread of crime. These anxieties sometimes lead to loneliness and isolation.

However, there may be a more damaging aspect of continual media bombardment. Four or five hours a day in front of the television leaves little time for personal interaction, whether it be with children, neighbors or friends. It certainly doesn't allow much time for participation in groups, churches, clubs or worthwhile organizations that do commendable work in the community. Nor does it allow time for assisting in youth sports and activities.

People say they are too busy to help out with what needs to be done at schools, churches and civic organizations. For some, work schedules and other obligations make volunteer work difficult. Others may have the time but not the inclination to participate.

Some psychologists believe that television can become addictive. For many viewers, the decision to do without TV for even a short time leads to withdrawal symptoms. Studies show that feelings of anxiety and restlessness are common, especially in the first few days, as individuals and family members adjust to the newfound free time without TV.

A more degrading development, affecting tens of millions of American men, is addiction to pornography. While available on television, it is pervasive on the internet, so much so that pornography pops up at times even when not desired or expected. Beautiful women and sex are appealing to men, and a billion dollar a year industry preys on their natural inclinations leading them to spend hours of wasted time and energy. The unlimited availability of porn means it can be turned on at any time. Unfortunately, those who become addicted to the portrayals of nonstop sex and the allure of voluptuous females may be setting themselves up for failure in the real world of male/female relationships.

Not only does television take up much of the free time of a great many American families, it is also a major means of acculturation. Many people discern what society is like by watching TV. How could it be otherwise? According to the Nielsen statistics, most people watch television more than they interact with anyone else. This is especially true for those whose work involves little public contact.

Is there a message that is imparted through our media, particularly through television? Yes, two clear messages are conveyed. The first is secularism. The second is consumerism.

Webster's definition of secularism is, "indifference to or rejection or exclusion of religion and religious considerations." Does television do this? Are you able to recall a TV show where a person entered a church and knelt down to pray? If so, it might have been in a very old movie. Alternatively, have you watched a family sit down to eat and say grace before the meal? Not likely. Have you heard any talk about sin, hell, the afterlife or of Christ dying for sins? Not likely, unless you have tuned to a specifically religious channel. Morality is almost never discussed on TV. This, despite the fact that most Americans profess Christianity.

The second major message that media stresses is consumerism. More than at any other time in the short history of television, we are continually bombarded with commercials. The time allotted for advertising on radio and television has more than doubled. In the 1960's, approximately 9 minutes of every television hour were set aside for advertising. Today, the time allotted for advertising is up to 22 or 24 minutes per hour leaving at most only 38 minutes of programming. A Wikipedia article states that in a ten hour period, Americans see approximately three hours of advertising. This does not include banner ads, the narrow streamers that often run at the bottom of the regular picture.

It appears that Americans have the dubious honor of watching the most advertizing on TV. Other countries, for the most part, enjoy much less interruption of programming for commercial purposes. Generally, it is an agency of the government that limits advertising, though in some countries, as the Philippines, their Association of Broadcasters regulates ad time.

Some Americans have had enough. They are taking steps to see programming without the interruptions. They record shows or games and then fast forward through all the commercials and timeouts. It is surprising how short a basketball game is when you remove everything not part of the game. Others take an even simpler approach. They mute the TV during commercials. Often, there is plenty of time to read the paper or a good book during all the interruptions.

There is no doubt that corporations spend enormous amounts of money on advertising to bring their products to our attention. During prime time, ads often cost hundreds of thousands of dollars for a thirty second commercial. Ads run during the Super Bowl may cost millions. And that is only for the air time. The cost of paying professional advertising companies to produce the ads may be substantially more.

We notice that companies are buying the right to name baseball, football and basketball stadiums. Few seem to complain. We live in a capitalistic country and realize it is all about money. Most sports figures make millions; someone has to pay them. Unrecognized is the effect of constant advertising on our mental outlook—on our personalities.

Why are companies willing to disburse so much money? Especially when many people say they pay no attention to advertising? Nevertheless, the average adult and child sees more than 20,000 ads a year. The sole purpose of commercials is to get people to buy something. Are they successful? The short answer is, they must be. How else can corporations justify the tremendous cost of air time?

Companies know that through advertising they can influence people's buying of trucks, cars, beer, clothes, medicine, computers, phones, vacuum cleaners, jewelry, movie and theater tickets, etc. They encourage us to buy things we don't need by focusing on how we can keep up with the Jones—or show them up. Ads tell us "Just do it," "you're worth it," and, "you owe it to yourself," to break down any reservations we may have about making a new purchase.

Commercials depict how various medications and preparations can restore health, eliminate wrinkles, and regrow hair, etc, quickly passing over all the possible dangerous side effects. Much time and advertising dollars are spent telling men what beer to drink and how manly we would be if we owned a certain powerful pickup truck. Despite the constant barrage of ads, consumers know there is a limit to what can be purchased. Regardless of the allure advertisers create for their products, most of us realize we cannot have it all. Some don't, however, and the result is often massive credit card debt and even the loss of home through foreclosure.

Frequently, our defense is to become skeptical of advertising claims. Most of us have been burned when a product turns out to be not as good as advertised. Skepticism relating to the endless ads can easily become ingrained. The transition, from being skeptical about consumer products, to a generalized skepticism of life is probably not difficult in a consumer culture. It can become very easy to focus on faults of others, the bad weather, the poor economy, health problems, etc. than to appreciate the gifts God has given to each of us.

The practical necessity of doubting the claims of advertisers tends to carry over to our dealings with others. We are often quite suspect of claims made by strangers and have our doubts sometimes even of the accuracy of statements made by friends. When a person in authority speaks, be it a teacher, manager, minister, the pope or a politician—especially a politician, we tend to have our doubts.

Skepticism can become a way of life. The skeptic may seldom be fooled, but on the other hand, he or she may completely miss enjoyable things and amicable people. For skeptics, the cup is never half-full but always half empty. In today's society, it is quite easy to become so focused on what is wrong with individuals, organizations, and even Christianity, that we fail to see the good in people, institutions and the church.

Unfortunately, it is the lot of humans to make mistakes. It is safe to say that all humans do. Organizations make mistakes too, precisely because they are run by people. We notice when things don't seem right, and we note inconsistencies. At times, rather than complain, it may be worthwhile to step in and try to make a difference. The view from inside a group or organization is often quite different than that seen from the outside.

In sum, television, and in particular all the advertising on television, has the potential to make us skeptical people. If we turn away from God because of all the imperfections we see in the world, we turn away from the One who is Perfect, who invites us to live forever in a place without flaw–heaven.

Where Christianity is Growing

Those who believe in Jesus and who go to church may sometimes become dismayed at the apparent lack of faith of those around them. They may be aware that large numbers of people no longer attend services. The decline in the numbers of church going Christians is notable in Europe and in many parts of America.

Unrecognized by most Americans and Europeans is the veritable explosion of Christianity in other parts of the world. Anyone who believes that Christianity is undergoing a period of decline the world over is in for a surprise. Moreover, the following information should make it apparent that Christianity can no longer be thought of as the religion of the Western World.

Some surprising statistics are enumerated in the International Bulletin of Missionary Research, the mid 2011 edition. The following table is from their research.

Charting global religion (millions)

	1800	1900	1970	2000	2011
Christians	205	558	1,231	1,998	2,307
Muslims	091	200	581	1,294	1,578
Hindus	108	203	462	815	952
Buddhists	69	127	234	416	468
Jews	9	12	15	14	15

These numbers show the growth of religion with population increase since 1800. Not counted in the table are 658 million people with no religious affiliation and almost 140 million atheists. Their numbers are significant, but remain far below the billions of people worldwide who profess religious belief.

The next table illustrates the growth of Christianity by regions. It includes Christians of all types, that is, Catholics, Protestants, Orthodox, Independents, Anglicans and marginal Christians. Currently the largest of these is Catholics, with Independents and Protestants following. The Independent Churches do not adhere to the guidelines of any mainline church.

Christianity by region (millions)

	1800	1900	1970	2000	2011
Africa	4	9	116	357	475
Asia	8	21	92	275	354
Europe	172	368	467	548	559
Latin America	15	60	263	477	543
North America	6	60	168	212	231
Oceania	0	4	15	21	24

In 1800, Europe was home to the largest number of Christians in the world—172 million. By comparison, Latin America had 15 million and North America had 5.6 million Christians with another 8.3 million living in Asia.

Moving forward to 1900, European Christianity jumped to 368 million with Latin America and North America rising to roughly 60 million each. Africa at the time had almost 9 million and Asia 21 million Christians.

The big surprise is seen in the stats for the year 2000. In the hundred years since 1900, Christianity in North American almost quadrupled to 212 million and in Europe rose to 548 million. However, Christianity in Africa skyrocketed from 9 million to 357 million and in Latin America multiplied from 60 million to 477 million!

By the year 2000, Latin America and Africa were rapidly gaining on Europe. As the latest figures from mid 2011 show, Latin America has substantially narrowed the lead of European Christianity. Projections indicate that by 2025 both Latin America and Africa will surpass Europe by a large margin. It is quite conceivable that by that date, there will be an African or Latin American pope.

A similar growth has been experienced in Asia, which includes the countries of China, Japan, India, Pakistan, Indonesia, Vietnam, Thailand, North and South Korea, Turkey and the Middle East, etc. From nearly 21 million Christians in 1900, as of 2011 there are now an estimated 354 million. Part of this growth is the result of missionary efforts, but much of it is the spread of faith through personal evangelization.

That Christianity is also growing in China may be surprising because it is a Communist country. Nevertheless, even though officially atheistic, the Chinese government's own estimate of the numbers of Christians has recently been listed at 20 million. Other, unofficial estimates, range from about 50 million to as many as 130 million. In a country of approximately one and one third billion people, 130 million would be approximately one tenth of the population.

The reason no one knows the total for sure is because many Christians in China do not register their religious affiliation with the authorities. There is fear that to do so would give the government control over the direction and the focus of faith. It is widely known that given the limited number of state authorized Catholic and Protestant churches, many Christians meet regularly in "house churches."

To date, the Chinese government has permitted these small assemblies to meet, as long as the number in attendance is twenty-five or less. When one of the small congregations gets too large, another home is added as a house church to facilitate the growing number of Christians. There is a remarkable similarity in China to the conditions prevalent in the Roman Empire when Christianity was a forbidden religion.

What is the nature of the Christianity that is enjoying phenomenal growth across the globe? Is it similar to what we find in the United States and Europe? Many of the denominations are the same. One finds Catholics, Lutherans, Baptists, Anglicans, Presbyterians, Pentecostals, etc.— most of the varieties of religion that are found in the West. However, there are differences.

The main difference a visitor would immediately notice in many if not most congregations is the intensity of the faithful, as expressed by their singing, their enthusiastic participation in ceremony, and their willingness to travel long distances, usually on foot, to attend services.

One might also note the general youthfulness of the congregations. Christianity seems to have captured the heart and imagination of the young, though, of course, older people attend as well. The generally high birth rates insure youthful demographics.

A significant difference found in non Western Christianity is the emphasis on healing and gifts of the spirit. It is evident that the growing churches in Africa, Latin America, China and Indonesia have focused closely on New Testament spirituality. For most of these churches, whether Roman Catholic, Baptist, Anglican, Pentecostal, or other, a strong belief in healing both of mental and physical ailments is pervasive. These churches take literally Luke's Gospel, Chapter Nine: "He summoned the Twelve and gave them power and authority over all demons and to cure diseases, and he sent them to proclaim the kingdom of God and to heal."

For many European and American churches, the age of miracles ended sometime after the Middle Ages, probably with The Enlightenment, or Age of Reason. Miraculous events are still linked to saints, but the ability of Christ's followers today to effect healing is generally not recognized. In a cultural milieu where every unknown event requires a *scientific* explanation, the expectation for anything miraculous is generally lacking.

Not so in the growing and developing countries now embracing Christianity. Not only do they believe in the relevance of miracles, they also take to heart Christ's words in Mark 16:17: "These are the signs that will be associated with believers: in my name they will cast out devils; they will have the gift of tongues; they will pick up snakes in their hands and be unharmed should they drink deadly poison; they will lay their hands on the sick, who will recover."

In sum, a majority of the fast growing Christian churches of non Western culture appear to have taken to heart the earlier understanding of faith found in the New Testament and the Acts of the Apostles. They view miracles and healing as entirely possible and likely. They are comfortable with speaking in tongues and the concomitant interpretation of tongues.

Even in Western nations, there is some recognition of the value of prayer for healing. Especially in life and death situations, cancer for example, people commonly ask for prayers. Maybe this is because we still don't have any surefire cure for the disease. When what doctors can do is limited, faith filled Christians usually pray. It may be surprising to some, but prayer does bring results.

A number of studies have tried to measure the beneficial outcomes of having people pray for cancer and heart patients. Usually, those in the prayed for populations have better medical results than those not receiving prayer. Not always, however. While most people with Christian convictions prefer to have prayers said for them, others do not. Those who do not may see invocation as the last resort. Their feeling may well be, "There is nothing that can be done for me medically, so now they are praying for me. I am doomed to die." Such an attitude regarding prayer may well be self fulfilling.

Unanswered Questions

At the beginning of this short book some questions were posed. Some of these have been answered. It is evident that worldwide Christianity is enjoying remarkable growth. The increases in Africa and South America are astounding, and even China is becoming more and more Christian.

In Europe, however, their appears to be a decline in the faithful, at least in the numbers of those who regularly attend religious services. Further diminishing the numbers of those professing Christianity is the continuing decline in the population of most European countries. Birth rates are so low that some countries are giving cash bonuses for having children. In addition, paid maternity leaves of from several weeks to well over a year are the norm. In fact, a

2004 study, updated in 2007 at Harvard and McGill universities surveyed 177 countries and found only four–the United States, Liberia, Papua New Guinea and Swaziland not offering paid maternity leave.

In America, rates of church attendance are below those of thirty years ago, though most American still profess some type of Christianity. If there is an actual decline in belief, it is much smaller than in Europe. Many Protestant churches have seen declines in numbers in the last ten and twenty years. On the other hand, evangelical and Pentecostal churches have registered solid gains.

The Catholic Church in America has seen much fluctuation in the last few decades. The church has seen a loss of almost a third of those who were raised Catholics, yet the proportion of Americans who are Catholic remains at approximately 25% of the population. This comes at a time when the Protestant proportion has declined and those who have no church affiliation has risen.

There are two reasons why there are more Catholics in the United States than before in total numbers, as well as the same 25% of the population.

The first is that the church continues to attract a fair number of converts. The second and major reason is a large percentage of immigrants coming into the country are Catholic. This is particularly true of former Latin American residents, the largest immigrant group coming from Mexico.

The need for faith

To some extent, people who live a comfortable lifestyle, who are not troubled by war, the prospect of famine or insecure old age may be able to live without faith. Their lives may not be enriched, but they can survive. In the most highly developed countries of the world, the necessities of life are taken care of by the state. Many Western countries have healthcare plans, welfare, social security and unemployment compensation, etc. Diseases that used to kill half the children before they reach maturity have largely been eliminated or controlled by vaccination. In the United States, the death of a mother in childbirth, fairly common before modern medicine, is today almost unheard of.

It is easy for people now, especially youth, to feel "invincible," in the sense that nothing can go wrong. Some shrug off advice to be careful, to slow down on the highway, and to wait before becoming intimate. As noted earlier, our media, particularly advertising, tells us not to hold back, to give in to our desires, and to "go for the gusto."

It seems that most of today's movies, other than those for children, feature first date sex, often along with offensive language, violence and drugs. An old study from the 80's conducted by Lichter and Rothman determined that media people don't share the religious values of the US population. They are far more likely to favor abortion, and they are much more acceptable of both adultery and homosexual lifestyles.

Advertisers, of course, want to sell their products, The more we buy the happier they are. They are decidedly not in the business of coaching us on the correct or moral way. In fact, the opposite is more likely to be the case.

In sum, our medical and social systems that help to protect us from danger can indeed provide us with a false sense of security. When we don't have to worry about our job, our health, or our next meal, it becomes easy to forget how much we owe to God's bounty. We can easily take everything for granted.

Forgotten is Christ's life of healing the sick—the impetus for care centers and later for hospitals that we now take for granted. Forgotten is role of the church in saving and promoting knowledge, at first through the monasteries and then in the founding and staffing of schools. Without education there would be no science, and without the civilizing power of Christianity we might well still be in the early dark ages where magic, strong man rule, and personal insecurity was the norm. A time when normal life expectancy was only thirty to forty-five years. These same conditions are present in parts of Africa today.

We owe much to Christianity, to Jesus Christ. Nevertheless, our current freedoms must be preserved against powerful interests that would dismantle our hard won gains. There is evil in the world and not only terrorists are to be feared. Witness what happened to the Christian nation of Germany when Hitler came to power. Not only were 6,000,000 Jews killed, but millions of other Germans died in war and the bombings, leaving Germany a shattered nation.

The assistance of a Christian nation, the United States, through the Marshall Plan, also known as the European Recovery Program, played a major role in helping the hard working Germans and other European nations rebuild their countries.

Belief in miracles

As we know, during Christ's ministry, and in the early years of the Church, miracles were common. They have always been a standard belief within the Catholic Church, and today two are required before the pope can pronounce a person a saint.

It is certainly not only Catholics who believe in miracles. Other Christian faiths do, as well as Muslims. The Catholic Church does seem to have a monopoly on the investigation and authentication of miracles due to its hierarchical structure.

What is apparent now, even though the age of miracles in the early church is long since past, is that there is a rising incidence of miracles occurring in Christianity in developing countries. This boom in miracles is taking place in both Catholic and Protestant faith traditions.

We don't see this nearly as much in America and in Europe where our much higher standard of living and availability of modern medicine and trained doctors permits putting faith in technology.

Certainly nothing in Christianity, in Christ's message, is opposed to utilizing the latest technology and skills of trained physicians. The point has been made, after all, that science is an outgrowth of education fostered by Christianity.

Nevertheless, in time, most of us come to realize there are limits to what a doctor can do. Furthermore, we are aware that hospitals and surgery centers sometimes harbor virulent infections.

Therefore, earnest prayer for God's help in all situations of need, whether it be a child's sickness, that of a friend, or our own well-being is to be encouraged. Christians believe God's power is unlimited. However, He will not work in the absence of faith. Perhaps, because of skepticism, we miss out on God's bounty. Maybe we, like the father in scripture who asked for the cure of his son, could also say, "I do believe, help my unbelief!" (Mark: 9:24)

Belief in God and Science

The focus of this short book has been Christianity and culture. The majority of people in the world adhere to some form of religion. However, there is a substantial minority with no particular religious belief. Having been raised a Catholic, there are many aspects of faith I personally questioned. The simple answer given me was usually, "You have to have faith." I can accept that answer now better than then.

However, those who have no religion, is it simply because they have not received faith? Is faith a gift from God? A person who was raised in a household with no religion, or worse, raised by those who believe religious belief is evil, will likely have a hard time accepting faith. This, through no fault of their own. Yet we know that even Indians in our own country, who had no knowledge of

Christ, nevertheless had religious beliefs. It is definitely conceivable that a person through no fault of their own might be lacking in faith. However, despite its absence, such a person would nevertheless have a sense of right and wrong.

Those of us who are Christians do have faith, and we believe God does love us to an astonishing degree. We appreciate his love, and in our better moments we try to be loving as well in imitation of him. At times, we may feel suffused with the spirit of God. We may feel God's presence in an intimate way.

To an atheist this personal love of God may be hard to understand. However, it should be noted that there is much that remains a mystery, even at the ordinary, naturalistic level. For example, how can we grasp the findings of astronomy that the known universe consists of one to ten septillion stars, many with planets circling them? Intuitively, it seems, we recognize that so much matter could not have simply come about without some sort of creation.

Gravity too, remains a mystery. Gravity is a force that is everywhere. It causes the stars, including our sun, to shine, and it keeps the planets in orbit. Though scientists don't really understand gravity, our world and the universe could not exist without it. We are personally affected by gravity; it pulls us constantly to the earth and causes us to weigh a specific number of pounds on a scale. There is nothing we can do to get away from gravity other than travel to the moon. There, our weight would be far less because the moon has one-sixth the mass of the earth. We believe in gravity, but we don't understand it.

Similarly, the relatively new findings of quantum mechanics and the nature of the atom are difficult to comprehend. The hard particles, atoms, envisioned by Democritis long ago were accepted as true until scientists discovered there is much more to the atom. Now, we realize that the content of the atom is essentially empty space, and only the movement of the electrons around the protons and neutrons keeps our bodies and the universe in existence. Without the waves of energy that represent the motion of electrons, we would collapse into something so tiny as not to be seen. What (Who) keeps everything in motion?

There also remains much we don't know about the universe, though modern science is able to give us some insights. Albert Einstein's theories on time and matter have been proven to be accurate, and we now know that time is relative. Time passes slower for astronauts moving at high speed than it does for people on earth. If a person could travel at near the speed of light for a month, on returning he or she would find all friends and relatives long dead. Most physicists believe that time began when the universe was formed. For a being not bound by the matter of the universe, there is no time at all. How events can happen in sequence in the absence of time is something we do not understand. Nevertheless, if heaven and hell are outside of time it is not surprising that they will last forever.

Scientists are only beginning to understand how the mind might have some control over matter. Yet with faith, Jesus and his disciples repeatedly cured the sick.

Today, in medicine, there is an increasing awareness of the mind's ability to influence the body. Doctors have known for decades that placebos, inert tablets given in place of a medication, have a surprising ability to produce curative effects in patients. These results have been thoroughly documented. Yet it is known that since there is no active ingredient in the pill, it is the patient's belief—his or her mental state, or *faith*, that causes the cure. The opposite is also true. Patients have been falsely diagnosed with terminal cancer and have proceeded to die even though they didn't have a trace of malignancy.

It is clear from the above and from a wealth of other evidence that the mind has a powerful effect on the body. Psychologists have long known that an optimistic attitude toward life is itself beneficial to health and well-being. It is also known that attitude is important for healing. A patient who trusts his doctor and the methods he or she is using is far more likely to recover than one who is skeptical. The need for faith was true even in Christ's time. Mark's gospel states: ". . . he could work no miracle there [Nazareth]. . ." (Mark 6:5) It is not surprising that people in Christ's hometown lacked faith in him. He was known to them as a carpenter, not a prophet and healer-miracle worker.

Bibliography

Barrow, John, D. *The Artful Universe,* Clarendon Press, Oxford, England, 1995.

Daniel-Rops, Henri, *Daily Life in the Time of Jesus,* Servant Books, Ann Arbor, MI, 1961

Darling, David, *Equations of Eternity,* Hyperion, New York, 1993.

Glynn, Patrick, *God The Evidence. The Reconciliation of Faith and Reason in a Postsecular World*, Forum, Rocklin, CA. 1999.

Jenkins, Philip, *The Next Christendom–The coming of Global Christianity,* Oxford University Press, New York, 2007.

Le Roy Ladurie, Emmanuel, *Montaillou, The Promised Land of Error,* Vintage Books, New York, 1979 edition.

Mander, Jerry, *Four Arguments for the Elimination of Television,* Quill, New York, 1978.

Mattingly, Terry, *Pop Goes Religion—Faith in Popular Culture,* W Publishing Group, Nashville, TN, 2005.

McCutcheon, Marc, *Everyday Life in the 1800's,* Writer's Digest Books, Cincinnati, OH, 1993.

Moreland, J.P., *Kingdom Triangle,* Zondervan, Grand Rapids, MI, 2007.

Schmidt, Alvin, J. *How Christianity Changed the World,* Zondervan, Grand Rapids, MI, 2004.

Schroeder, Gerald, L. Ph.D. *Genesis and the Big Bang,* Bantam Books, New York, 1990.

Stark, Rodney, *The Rise of Christianity,* HarperCollins, San Francisco, 1997.

Stromberg, Roland, N. *European Intellectual History since 1790,* Prentice Hall, 1993.

Wilson, Derek, *Charlemagne,* Doubleday, New York, 2006.

Various contributing writers, *After Jesus—The Triumph of Christianity,* Readers Digest, Pleasantville, NY, 1992.

Other books by Tom Molnar

Nonfiction

A Quick Look at Heaven

Included in this book, but available separately for individual or classroom use. Amazon, $2.99.

Discovering Mary, the Mother of Jesus

A realistic look at Mary, the Jewish girl who was chosen to become the mother of God. A view of her life, joys and sorrows as she came to know, better than anyone, the true message of her son. Forthcoming.

Fiction

Dark Age Maiden

Since the tragedy that destroyed his family, Uberto has lived by his sword and his wits. He wants full knighthood and the hand of the not easily won Lady Carina. Two things stand in his way: Count Giancarlo, a renowned sword fighter, and the Muslim invasion of France.

Lady Carina has thoughts of her own. She has boldly turned town her father's choice for marriage. Now, she finds herself sought by a gallant knight and a wealthy count. Before long, she comes to know the power of love. But is it too late? Large paperback, 220 pages. At Amazon. *$8.99*

Love Stories from the Heart

Warmhearted short fiction about both ordinary and out of the ordinary people. Large paperback, 103 pages. *$5.99*
At Amazon.

Bridestar

Far in the future, an inhabited planet is found–with a land and a love worth fighting for. Large paperback, forthcoming.

A Quick Look at Heaven

and Hell

A view unlike any we might imagine

Tom Molnar

Apple Valley Press

Manufactured in the United States of America.

ISBN 978-0-9766952-1-9

Contents

Prologue

Chapter One: The Age of Faith and beyond.

Chapter Two: The creation of man.

Chapter Three: Questionable images of heaven.

Chapter Four: In the body or out of the body?

Chapter Five: What does the Bible really say about heaven?

Chapter Six: Near death descriptions of heaven.

Chapter Seven: What we will do there—it won't be boring.

Chapter Eight: Fire and brimstone?

Chapter Nine: Who actually goes there?

Conclusion

From the back cover

Few know what heaven will be like, yet most people hope to go there. Misconceptions abound, making it hard to know what to expect. Some common views of eternity are disturbing for those who are actively involved in the bustle and satisfactions of life. Fortunately, many of the old notions can now be laid to rest. Drawing from scriptural passages, scientific advances, and life after death experiences, we can come to grips with a heaven that is both exciting and fulfilling.

Prologue

Many scientists who were formerly atheists or agnostics are turning back to God. One reason for this is the recent scientific discoveries making it difficult not to believe in a Creator. Unfortunately, most people are not aware of these discoveries. They are not taught in high school. Yet they verify what people of faith have always believed—that God made the universe.

Most believe that God, or some creative force, was necessary to start the universe. The question of this Being's current activity in creation is debated. Is God still active? Or did the One who began it all leave creation to develop on its own? Is it possible that, once started, the whole of creation came about through evolutionary processes? Or, on the other hand, has God been active in his creation and in fact in the lives of people today? People who pray certainly expect results. Why pray if no results are forthcoming? We commonly hear the words, "My prayers were answered." Does this mean that God is active in the lives of people and thus active in creation? We will consider the evidence.

The most complex creation of all is life. Plants, animals and especially man—beings that grow and move and communicate, are much more complex than the largest star or planetary system. The processes of life that sustain us—our circulatory, nervous, respiratory and parasympathetic systems are amazingly intricate, and to this day not fully understood. Our individual DNA makes each of us unique and guides our growth from the time of conception to adulthood. Of all the forms of life, human beings are the most endowed. With our brains we rule the world. We create wonderful music and magnificent works of art and technology. No other creature on earth compares with us. We see the world in full color, not in black and white or in a limited palette like most animals. Even in sex, we have privilege. Unlike animals, man and woman face each other and are not limited to a certain time of the year when the female is in heat.

What lies beyond? When our time on earth is finished what will happen to us? Some say there is nothing after death. Most of us, however, believe in an afterlife. But what kind? We don't often speak about the future life. In Western culture the focus is on the here and now or on the near future. Speculation on life after death is not currently in vogue. Perhaps because it requires thinking about our death. Fear of death seems ingrained in our culture. We try to look younger and act younger while enjoying the good things of life. Eternity can wait.

Death can be difficult or it can be peaceful. Unless our demise comes quickly, as in a fatal heart attack or auto collision, it can be hard for us to let go of the good things of life. Fear of the unknown, of the afterlife itself, can be stressful. If we know what to expect, perhaps we might accept our eventual death with peace. Regrettably, our knowledge of the afterlife is often quite limited. We may have patently false expectations that make us cringe.

Fortunately, there is a wealth of information about life after death. The most traditional is scripture based. This can be enlightening for those who have faith in inspired writings—mainly Christians, Jews and Muslims. Other information about the afterlife comes from scientific discoveries and near death experiences. These other sources appear to validate and give additional insight to biblical passages.

In truth, we cannot know everything about what is to come. Many aspects of heaven and hell must remain unknown. Nevertheless, it is surprising how much we can learn about what to expect in the future. Technical changes and research is making it easier for us to get the information we are seeking. Before describing the new developments, let's take a brief look at how the traditional views of heaven and earth were drastically altered by scientific findings.

Chapter One

The Age of Faith and beyond

The Age of Faith in Europe, over a thousand years long, was brought to an end in the Sixteenth Century by the Reformation and the astronomer Copernicus. The Age began with Constantine's Edict of Milan in 313 AD, which granted religious freedom for Christians within the Roman Empire. When Rome subsequently grew weaker and lost political importance in the next two centuries, the Church emerged by default as the only influential organization left in Europe.

Beginning with St. Benedict, early in the sixth century, major monasteries began to be founded all over Europe. They were centers of spirituality whose members took vows of poverty, chastity and obedience. They also provided accommodations for travelers and care for the sick. The Monks laboriously copied by hand the classical books of Greece and Rome. The monasteries provided the only education that existed in the early Middle Ages. Sons of nobility learned Latin, logic, rhetoric, philosophy, mathematics and, of course, religion—the same education as those who would become priests. By the ninth century, Charlemagne, realizing the need for learning, decreed that every cathedral should also establish a school. The cathedral schools later developed into some of the great universities of Europe.

It is likely that the strong influence of the Roman Church in the Middle Ages created the religious mind set of the time. Although most of the people lived in simple one or two room dwellings, they took pride in their church. By the tenth century, after the scourge of the Viking invasions had ended, much of Europe began building churches. Competition and hometown pride motivated the residents of even small towns to erect beautiful structures at the cost of many years of hard labor. It was not forced labor, however, but work both the poor and wealthy saw as giving glory to God—and no doubt assuring a place in paradise.

The emphasis on religious thought continued into the Renaissance. Today, most of the large galleries of the world contain major rooms of art from the fourteenth through the sixteenth centuries. The themes of Renaissance art dealt largely with faith, but for the first time religious subjects began to be painted in a completely different way. Realism in art blossomed in the late Middle Ages. The paintings of the virgin mother and child and the saints and apostles we still enjoy so much today are portraits of individuals. Representing religious subjects, they are the people of Europe captured by the great artists of the day. They are painted with a skill and naturalness that makes them come alive.

It was relatively easy during the Middle Ages to believe in God. Before Copernicus, most people thought heaven was directly above the earth, and God and all his saints and angels were there too. Those who looked at the world with eyes of faith saw miracles as an explanation for things they didn't understand. Just as we in our age look for scientific explanations for events, Middle Age people saw unexplainable events as the work of God, angels or demons. They believed that God and his son, Jesus, were physically close and concerned about man.

Then, in 1543, Copernicus, published his book, *On The Revolutions Of The Celestial Spheres*. No longer was the earth envisioned as the center of the universe with the sun going around it. The reverse was true. When Galileo, with his newly invented telescope proved Copernicus right, he was imprisoned. Though his sentence was commuted to house arrest, his books were banned. His finding that the earth was not at the center of the universe was troubling not only to church officials, but to most people. It was unsettling to learn that God was not directly overhead looking after humanity.

Galileo was only the first of innumerable scientists whose findings visualized the universe in ways that left God almost completely out of the picture. Scientific instruments cannot see God, and so He became a nonentity in the universe the new science was discovering. The borders of the universe were continually being pushed further and further away with the development of powerful telescopes. Not only did scientists discover that our sun is just another star among many thousands of billions, but astronomers would later learn that our own galaxy, the Milky Way, is but one of billions of galaxies.

Prior to the twentieth century, most people had little more than an elementary education. By the 1950's, high school education was afforded to almost everyone in the United States. With the concurrent rise of mass media through radio and television, scientific knowledge entered the mainstream of consciousness. At the same time, religious skepticism seemed to be on the rise in the Western World. On April 8th, 1966, the cover of Time Magazine asked, "Is God Dead?" For many atheists He *was* dead—killed by science.

Discussion questions

1. During the Middle Ages people saw God and the saints as being close—physically near. What is your perception of God's distance or nearness to mankind?

2. Scientists, with all their instrumentation, cannot see God. How might a person of faith be able to "see" God?

Chapter Two

The creation of man

At the very time the debate was raging over the existence of God, a revolution in scientific thinking was taking place. This revolution invalidates many of the theories that had relegated God to the sidelines. In fact, the new discoveries place God once again at the very center of the universe. Human beings, too, are recognized to have a much higher value in the order of creation. Based on the new scientific evidence, many thoughtful people contend that the universe was created purposely for man. Because of the new findings, not only people of faith, but also scientifically minded people are once again able to see God at the center of the universe.

What is this new information? What are the scientific discoveries that put God at the forefront? The following ancient biblical verse describes the creation of man:

"Yahweh God shaped man from the soil of the ground and blew the breath of life into his nostrils, and man became a living being."
(Genesis 2, verse 7.)

This simple way of describing man's creation is part of the ancient oral tradition of the Jews. It was put into writing about 1400 years before the Christian era, long before instruments for observing the universe were invented.

Man is indeed made from the material of the earth, as are all creatures. In death, his body returns to again become part of the earth. The infusion of life into inert matter does seem to be the province of God. Despite innumerable attempts, and a plethora of equipment, scientists have been unable to create life. Someday, with more advanced instrumentation, scientists may one day be able to rearrange already existing DNA and inject matter into an empty cell that may possibly reproduce. Even with advanced technology, however, creating life from scratch is extremely unlikely. That it could have arisen on its own seems even more improbable.

The conditions necessary for life do not start with earth. Life needs the universe. Scientists know that our own personal star, the sun, did not come into existence at the beginning of creation. Our sun is a second or third generation star, one that condensed from gasses and matter that were hurled into space when preexisting large stars exploded in supernovas. The immense heat and pressure within those stars created the elements necessary for life. The stuff of life and of our bodies—calcium, carbon, oxygen, nitrogen, and the iron in our blood were formed in the cauldron of first generation stars.

A contentious debate is currently going on in many areas of the country between evolutionists and adherents of Intelligent Design. Evolutionists believe that life evolved from the simplest one-celled creatures to all the variety in life we see today, including man. For evolutionists, life is a haphazard process, occurring by chance through genetic mutations over millions of years. Although direct fossil evidence leading to man, horses, and bats, etc. haven't been found, evolutionists remain confident that the evolutionary process explains the diversity of life on our planet.

Advocates of Intelligent Design, on the other hand, believe the complexity of life—including DNA, could only have come about through the intervention of a Creator.

The discovery of DNA in 1953 is a good example of life's intricacy. At conception, the combination of two cells, a sperm and an egg, creates an individual's entire DNA. From that point on, as the fertilized egg develops into a baby and then a man or woman, each facet of physical development is controlled by the information contained in the two original cells. Our skin tone, height, color of eyes and hair, facial features, as well as the layout of our internal organs, glands, muscles and nervous system are regulated by our DNA. The almost unlimited combinations of DNA means that everyone is different, with the exception of identical twins. The genetic data found in our DNA is recognized to be an extremely important identifier and has led to the release of inmates long imprisoned for crimes they did not commit.

Another important discovery of the twentieth century was the finding of the astronomical "red shift." Prior to the 1970's most scientists believed the universe was in a "steady state" condition. Since then, the discovery of cosmic background radiation and the finding that distant stars and galaxies are all moving away from us, and from each other, has totally changed our understanding of the universe. These observations have led most astronomers to the conclusion that the entire known universe resulted from an explosion—now called the "big bang."

For many people, big bang theory lends credence to a Creator—Someone who started the universe. Scientists have more recently learned that not just any bang would do, that the explosion from a tiny source of incredible energy had to be guided by incredibly fine tuning of the four basic forces of nature—the strong force, the electromagnetic force, the weak force and gravity. Scientists calculate that had any of these forces been off by even a fraction of a percent the earth would not exist. For those interested, there is a wealth of evidence for Intelligent Design, and many books have been written describing the multitudes of remarkably fortuitous conditions making life possible.

This book is not a scientific exposition. Anyone desiring to learn more about DNA, the forces of nature, Intelligent Design, the "big bang," and evolution will find entire books that delve into these subjects. The significance of these two opposing theories may lie more in their implications. Evolutionists may tend to regard the world differently than those who see God's hand in creation.

Let's take a look at evolutionary theory first. The full title of Darwin's first book is, *Origin of Species by Natural Selection, or the Preservation of Favored Races in the Struggle for Life*. Darwin postulated in this book that random mutations cause changes within organisms. The organisms compete to survive and reproduce, and those most successful at reproduction leave the most offspring. Over a long time period, a new species can evolve.

Evolutionary theory obviously leaves everything to chance. A god is not needed to create the tremendous diversity we see on earth. There is no need for a supreme being to be active in the world and certainly no evidence for belief in an afterlife. "We are on our own, left to our own devices, so make the most of it," or words to that effect, is advice that seems to follow naturally from evolutionary theory. Strict evolutionists do not perceive that a god is active in the universe, nor do they espouse a God-given standard of right and wrong. Our existence in the present time as thinking, animated creatures is totally due to chance.

Intelligent Design theorists, on the other hand, are unable to apprehend how the universe as we know it developed in the absence of an extremely intelligent creator. For them, the minute tolerances necessary for a universe able to sustain life are far too critical. The diversity of life, from amoebas to dinosaurs, to birds, mammals and man, in Intelligent Design theory requires intervention. The upshot of ID theory is that the Designer is active in his creation, and by extension, active in his greatest creation—man. Believers of Intelligent Design may see the world in all its beauty as a gift, carefully designed for life and for us. A sense of wonder and appreciation, even faith, is supported by the Intelligent Design model. Even without religious insight, an afterlife is a possible assumption. Since proponents of Intelligent Design see the Creator as still active in His universe, anything is conceivable—including a personal, caring God.

Discussion questions

1. What is your take on the evolutionary belief that millions of years ago, through natural processes, life evolved from inert matter?
2. How is it that each of us has a sense of right and wrong?
3. Many scientists believe man evolved from apes. What is your view, and does your view include any direct action on God's part in man's creation?

Chapter Three

Questionable images of heaven

Belief in an afterlife has a long history. Archeological evidence shows pre-historic ritual burial practices from the Neolithic period, about (10,000—3,000 BC) as well as among Cro-Magnon humans (40,000—10,000 BC) and Neanderthals (100,000—28,000 BC.) The decoration of bodies, and the burying of useful items next to the corpse supports a primitive belief in life after death.

Almost all historical cultures, some more than others, are concerned with life in the future. The Egyptians, in particular, built monumental pyramids to house the dead and included their possessions for use in the next life. Not only the pharaohs, but anyone with money had their deceased preserved for the afterlife by mummification. For Greeks and Romans, Hades was the place of the dead. Though usually depicted as dark and shadowy, in time, Romans came to believe Hades was also a land of happiness for those who had lived rightly.

Two of the major world religions, besides Christianity and

Judaism, are Hinduism and Buddhism. These religions both envision numerous reincarnations until enough good karma is achieved and the human life force finally enters into "the kingdom of inexhaustible light." The beliefs of American Indians of both North and South America are varied, but a commonly held view is a pleasant afterlife where ordinary activities continue in a place sometimes specifically named "The Happy Hunting Ground."

In our own time, many different views of the afterlife exist. Some, like the following, seem rather implausible.

Harps, halos and clouds

The image of changeless perfection, billowing white clouds and a timelessness where nothing exciting happens is a common belief. The soft pluck of harp strings and abstract spirituality seems out of step with the spirit of human beings who thrive on excitement and challenge. Such a heaven may not be what God has planned for us.

Disembodied spirits singing praises to God.

Awareness of the decomposition of the body may lead to envisioning heaven as a nonmaterial place. Such a heaven may be easier for us to imagine, but is such a description accurate? The difficulty of reassembling our bodies as they were on earth is challenging for man but not for God. He can put us back together again if He wishes. As intelligent beings, whose powers will be enhanced in paradise, we will have the opportunity to give praise to our creator in many different ways.

A place of rest and sleep.

Although we frequently hear, "May he or she rest in peace," heaven is not a place removed from activity and life. Instead, it is much more likely to be a place of joy and excitement. Our minds will be active, with far greater understanding than ever before. If we have physical bodies, they will be healthy and vigorous. Not that we won't have time for reflection, or for something akin to reading. Christ in John, 14 said, "In my Father's house there are many dwelling places, If there were not, would I have told you I am going to prepare a place for you?" It would appear that from the comfort of our own home we will be able to go out and delight in all the joys of heaven.

Discussion questions

1. Archeological evidence shows that man's belief in an afterlife is ancient–appearing even before recorded history. How would you describe your own outlook for life after death?
2. What might you personally look forward to in paradise?

Chapter Four

In the body or out of the body?

If you ask five people how they might experience heaven—in bodily form or as a spirit, you may get different answers. Most, in my experience, expect that if they make it to paradise they will be in the form of a spirit. Not too surprising. Even in the early church, there were some who did not believe in the resurrection. Nevertheless, as early as the Second Century AD, the Christian church affirmed in The Apostles Creed the resurrection of the body. The tenet is based on a number of scriptural passages, the strongest being the entire chapter fifteen in One Corinthians. Paul is quite clear that as Christ rose from the dead in bodily form, we also will likewise share in his glory.

In the present age, shaped as we are by a materialistic outlook and scientific progress, belief in the actual resurrection of the body, and not just the spirit, may be difficult. Yet we see life renew itself every spring, and those of us who garden trust that life will spring from the inert seed we plant in the ground. The seed contains a form of unseen life. For it to germinate it must die. Farmers and gardeners know that whatever they plant will grow true to the form of the seed type they have chosen.

Christians believe that at death the spirit lives on to be happy with God in paradise, or to be unhappy in hell. The resurrection of the body is to come later, at the end of the world and the second coming of Christ. Some may question how God can resurrect bodies that were long ago buried in the ground. Their atoms may now be anywhere—in trees, flowers, or at the bottom of the ocean. For a long time Christian churches condemned cremation because it destroyed the body. Their stance likely was influenced by the Roman persecutions, for sometimes the bodies of martyrs were burned or mutilated to prevent the possibility of resurrection.

God, of course, has no difficulty in resurrecting a body intact. Current knowledge of the nature of atoms makes this far easier for us to understand. In science classes, we learn that all atoms are alike; a hydrogen atom is like any other hydrogen atom, a carbon atom like any other carbon atom, etc. God's knowledge of our DNA is sufficient to put us back together exactly as we were.

But *would* we be like we were? There is much debate on the subject. When a child dies, does he or she come to heaven as a child? Similarly, does a person who dies at a ripe old age live in heaven as elderly? It is clear from scripture that there will be no illness, no deformity. It is also clear that our bodies will be glorified and immortal. (Philippians 3:20-21, 1 Corinthians 15:51-52)

Some theorize our age in heaven will be that of Christ when he died—about thirty-three. This might represent full maturity before the onset of old age.

Personally, I tend to think our bodies will be resurrected at our body's earliest fully mature age. Some say that is about twenty-four or twenty-five. Babies will likely come to heaven fully matured, and the elderly will again see the full bloom of youth. Time, after all, has no meaning in the afterlife. The ravages of age, the sagging of our skin, etc. caused by gravity will have no effect on our immortal bodies. (1 Corinthians 15:21-22 & 42-44, Revelation 21:4)

Discussion question

1. As we age, we come to realize that we can't do all the things we used to do. We all know it is hard to think clearly when we are tired. Things tend to upset us the most when we are weary. With sickness, we also find everything more difficult. Given fresh, immortal bodies, all that will change in heaven. Let's talk about that.

Chapter Five

What does the Bible really say about heaven?

In this section, we will look at what scripture can tell us about heaven. There is more in the Book than most people realize.

There are a great number of references to the afterlife in both the Old and the New Testament. One of the major statements is from Christ himself. When the apostles were gathered with Christ at the last supper Jesus told them he was going to leave them. As previously noted, He then comforted them with these words:

"In my Father's House there are many dwelling places. If there were not, would I have told you that I am going to prepare a place for you? And if I go and prepare a place for you, I will come back again and take you to myself, so that where I am you also may be." (John, 14).

It is evident from this that those who follow Christ are to rise to take the places He has prepared. Paul speaks at length in One Corinthians, section15 of how our bodies are also to be resurrected. In fact, he says, ". . .Christ has been raised from the dead, the first fruits of all those who have fallen asleep." Paul continues, saying, "For just as in Adam all die, so too in Christ shall all be brought to life. . ."

It is explicit from these two passages, as well as in many other places in the bible, that a *physical* resurrection is indicated. It also seems apparent that our body will share a likeness to the risen body of Christ. Food will not be necessary to our immortal bodies, yet like Christ after his resurrection, we will be able to eat. In fact, many biblical passages refer to those in paradise enjoying eating and drinking at "a heavenly banquet."

Not only will our perfected body again be united with our spirit, we are told we will also have our own physical place in heaven. Christ speaks of preparing "many dwelling places," and several other verses in scripture speak of a heavenly city. There, we will be given our own space, our home. How will it be decorated? Just the way we like it, for it is custom made for each of us. From our dwelling places, we will have freedom to go anywhere else and still be fully in God's presence.

It should be obvious that there will be no wickedness or evil in heaven. All *unrepentant* sinners will be excluded, and there will no need to be on guard with strangers as we are on earth. In fact, there will be no strangers in heaven. We will share with all a friendship grounded in the love of Christ in whose kingdom we belong. Our reunions with loved ones and new friends will encompass the full range of our intellectual and emotional makeup—we will not be less human in heaven but more. With real, physical bodies, we will embrace and welcome the caress of those we love. We may very well shed tears of joy. The nature of man remains the union of the soul and spirit with the material body.

Heaven does not change man's character. Our body, now incorruptible, will be united with our soul to live forever in eternity.

Will we be male and female? This question may best be answered in Genesis 1:27. "God created man in the image of himself; in the image of God he created him; male and female he created them." If it is true that our maleness and our femaleness reflects the image of the Creator, than it seems likely we will retain our masculinity and femininity. Christ himself, born a boy child, lived as a man, and after his resurrection appeared to the apostles and others as a man. Doubtless, we will retain our own God-given personalities in heaven, without our aberrant traits. Gender is certainly an important part of our personality.

An objection may be made by those familiar with scripture. It is true that when Christ was questioned by the Sadducees, who didn't believe in an afterlife, he answered that there is no marriage in heaven. He said nothing about gender. Nor did he say that there is not a special relationship in heaven between those who lived as man and wife on earth. Rather, he was answering the Sadducees complex question about a woman who married several men, each of whom died, as to whom she would be married to in heaven. It was the Sadducees way of trying to trap Jesus, since they did not believe in an afterlife. Jesus answered them, explaining that there is no marriage in heaven.

So far, we have not focused on what we will do in heaven. That is coming. First, let's examine another important source of information providing more insight into what heaven is like.

Discussion questions

1. Genesis, 1:27 says:

"God created man in his image;
in the divine image he created him;
male and female he created them"

What does it mean to you to be created in the image of God?

2. Jesus said he was going to prepare a place for the apostles. Do you think he will do that for us as well? If so, what kind of place do you think it might be?

Chapter Six

Near Death Descriptions of Heaven

Near death experiences, also termed out of the body experiences, have been reported for well over a hundred years. In modern times, when emergency medical procedures can save a person who would otherwise die, glimpses of the afterlife have become quite common. One estimate is that ten to fifteen percent of people rescued from death are able to describe a continued life away from the body. As a result, descriptions of near death experiences have become somewhat common and many books are written on the subject. After one reads numerous accounts of these experiences, certain recurring similarities become apparent.

At the point of death, the spirit departs from the physical body. At first, the person may not grasp that it is in fact his or her own body, because there is no longer any pain or bodily sensations. Usually, one's recognition of the body comes in a detached, non-emotional way.

A surprising aspect of near death experiences is the complete clarity of consciousness. In every account I have read, the passage from life to death does not cut off the awareness of the spirit. The mind is fully alert and the person is often able to describe dispassionately the people there as well as the machines being used in the attempt to bring the body back to life. Remarkably, even people who are blind have perfect vision in this state and can see what is going on as doctors and nurses work frantically to restore life.

The condition of those who have described their near death experience is almost invariably incorporeal. They often float briefly above their body watching the activities of the medical staff. Attempts to touch any of those present at the death scene are without effect. Outstretched hands and arms hold nothing, passing through any substance like a cloud. Quite often, it is at this point that the person leaves the scene of death, passing through walls and frequently experiencing something often described as "like a dark tunnel." This is not always the case. Some may immediately see a bright light. Those who *do* experience the tunnel usually see a light far in the distance. Moving through the tunnel, they are aware of both warmth and love emanating from the source of light.

Those who are Christian frequently come to a realization that it is an angel or even Jesus Christ himself who welcomes them to a new life. Most also feel that directly or indirectly their life on earth comes under review. They see very clearly the times they have hurt others and the morality of their actions. The good things they have done on earth also appear to pass before their eyes. Everything is perceived with vivid clarity. There is joy in witnessing good deeds and remorse in seeing the harm caused by sin. A feeling of overwhelming love is experienced by just about everyone who comes near the light. People express that words are inadequate to describe this feeling. Emanating from the being who welcomes them, is a love described as overpowering, pervasive and unconditional. Many feel embraced by the Lord.

In some near death experiences, there is a meeting with an important person one has known in life. He or she may be a grandparent, father, mother, or someone else who has preceded one in death. It is commonly this person who imparts the message that one must go back, who explains it is not the time to die and enter eternal life. In some near death experiences mention is made that the person seems much younger than when known on earth. In one man's account, he found to his surprise that his grandmother was "young and beautiful"

Discussion questions

1. Have you, or do you know someone who has had a near death experience? If so, what do you remember about it?

2. Books describing the experience of people, even children, in heaven continue to be popular. Some have become best sellers. What is your take on their authenticity?

2. In near death experiences, we see consciousness continuing after apparent death. What do you think is the significance of this for us?

Chapter Seven

What we will do there—it won't be boring.

Most people have little conception of what we will do for an eternity in heaven. A common belief is that we will pray and sing to give thanks to God. By itself, this conception of heaven is sufficient to turn many people off from wanting to go there. Such limited activities may not inspire people who are actively involved in a multitude of pursuits on earth.

Fortunately, this common belief is misleading. Heaven will be much more fun than we realize. It's true, of course, that we will give praise to God. That, and much more. According to scripture, we will have our bodies back again—strong, healthy bodies that will never know sickness united with our spirit that will leap with joy. There is no death, no problems or misunderstandings, no sorrow to make us despondent in heaven. It is likely that our bodies will also share the ability of Christ's resurrected body to pass through physical objects and to travel instantly across great distances. The bible in several places speaks of a "new heaven and new earth," which will replace the earth we know now. Revelation tells of a heavenly city of immense size. This could contain the "dwelling places" Christ speaks of that he is preparing for us.

Certainly we will enjoy meeting friends and loved ones in heaven. The relationships we formed on earth will no doubt be continued and deepened. Even though we will never again be hungry or thirsty in our immortal bodies, it seems we will enjoy eating and drinking. (Matthew 26:29, Isaiah 25:6, Revelation 19:9) We will likely marvel at the delightful taste of foods and enjoy drinks that are so far above soda, coffee, beer, wine and spirits that we will give praise to God for his bounty. Given that we will have real, immortal bodies, it is likely that we will also experience immense physical pleasure as well as emotional fulfillment far greater than any we have known on earth.

Will we travel to other galaxies to look at their wonders? It is possible. In fact, C.S. Lewis (author of *The Chronicles of Narnia, Mere Christianity, The Problem of Pain*, etc.) suggests we may be given the rule of a distant star. Several passages from scripture show that we will reign with Christ in heaven: (2 Timothy 2:12, Revelation 3:21 and 22:5, as well as 1 Corinthians 6:2-3.) It seems we will be given meaningful work to do which will utilize our creativity and God given abilities. Certainly, there is a reason why God created the billions of galaxies now known to exist, each with billions of stars, many perhaps with their own solar systems. There will be no lack of things for us to experience.

We will continue to learn—forever. Acquiring knowledge about all the works God has done for eternity will take eternity. Learning more about all the people we meet in paradise will also take forever. We will come to know people, not as acquaintances, but in depth, for there will be no secrets in heaven and no need to be selective about what we say. Our memories will be enhanced and we won't forget a name or face. No one in heaven will ever take advantage of us, so there will be no reason for anyone to be anything other than open and forthright. Chats with friends over refreshments will be warm and delightful.

All those we have helped on earth by our charitable giving and kind words will certainly look us up, and we will understand just how we made a difference in their lives. We too, will want to thank those who have helped us, and in heaven we will come to know them as friends.

Our main joy will be living with and being bathed in the personal love of Jesus Christ, the Father and the Holy Spirit. We will be overwhelmed by God's intimate connection with each of us. In paradise, we will finally begin to fully understand the depth of God's love. On earth, it is difficult to imagine the overflowing love of God because we ourselves are so limited. We tend to put restrictions on what God can do. That the creator of the universe could know and personally deeply love each individual he created is beyond our understanding. Yet in the Old Testament, psalm 139 speaks of God's intimate knowledge of each person:

"You formed my inmost being; you knit me in my mother's womb. Your eyes foresaw my actions; in your book all are written down. . ."

Discussion questions

1. If you arrived in heaven and could do anything you wanted to do, what do you think would be some of the first things you would like to do?

2. Several passages in scripture indicate that we will reign with God in heaven. Since we will retain our own individual talents, in fact, they will be enhanced, how might God utilize our talents in heaven?

Chapter Eight

Fire and Brimstone?

Not everyone will make it to heaven; we have it on good authority. Christ himself is very clear about hell. His words are in the Gospels. The visions of many saints concerning hell are also on record. Besides these sources, numerous near death experiences describe the terror of hell. Let's start our exploration of hell with the words of Christ, who actually spoke more about hell than he did about heaven.

". . .do not fear those who kill the body but are unable to kill the soul, but rather fear Him who is able to destroy both soul and body in hell." (Matt 10:28)

"You serpents, brood of vipers, how can you escape being condemned to hell?" (Matt 23:33)

". . .whoever says, 'You fool,' will answer for it in hell fire." (Matt 5:22)

"And if your eye should be your downfall, tear it out; it is better for you to enter into the kingdom of God with one eye than to have two eyes and be thrown into hell

where their worm will never die nor their fire be put out."
(Mark 9:47,48)

There are many other explicit teachings of Christ regarding hell, but perhaps the most dramatic is the story he told about the beggar Lazarus and the rich man in the Gospel of Luke. While on earth, Lazarus begged for the scraps from the rich man's table. Dogs came and licked his sores. After death, their circumstances are changed. The beggar is in heaven and the flames of hell torment the rich man. He begs Abraham to send Lazarus that he might have but a taste of water to cool his parched tongue. The complete story is in Luke 16:19-31.

Many people are aware of the Virgin Mary's appearances to the three children at Fatima, Portugal. In one of the apparitions, she showed them a vision of hell. Lucy, one of the children, later wrote of the experience:

". . .we saw, as it were, a vast sea of fire. Plunged in this fire, we saw the demons and the souls [of the damned]. The latter were like transparent burning embers, all blackened or burnished bronze, having human forms. They were floating about in that conflagration, now raised into the air by the flames which issued from within themselves, together with great clouds of smoke. Now they fell back on every side like sparks in huge fires, without weight or equilibrium, amid shrieks and groans of pain and despair, which horrified us and made us tremble with fright (it must have been this sight which caused me to cry out, as people say they heard me). The demons were distinguished [from the souls of the damned] by their terrifying and repellent likeness to frightful and unknown animals, black and transparent like burning coals."

As frightful as Lucy's description is, there are worse.

Some near death accounts are positively horrifying. The following account, told by a cardiologist who was trying to resuscitate a patient is particularly moving:

"Each time he regained heartbeat and respiration, the patient screamed, 'I am in hell!' He was terrified and pleaded with me to help him. I was scared to death. . . Then I noticed a genuinely alarmed look on his face. He had a terrified look worse than the expression seen in death! This patient had a grotesque grimace expressing sheer horror! His pupils were dilated, and he was perspiring and trembling—he looked as if his hair was 'on end.'"

" Then still another strange thing happened. He said, 'Don't you understand? I am in hell. . . Don't let me go back to hell!' . . .The man was serious and it finally occurred to me that he was indeed in trouble. He was in a panic like I had never seen before."

(Maurice Rawlings, *Beyond Death's Door*, (Thomas Nelson Inc., 1979) p. 3)

Other terrible near death experiences commonly describe going down into a deep pit, usually escorted by a felt but often-unseen presence of evil. Hearing the moans and screams of those who are tormented is common. Frequently there is witness of human bodies burning yet not being consumed by fire. Despite the flames, the scene described is usually darkened. Occasionally the experience is of cold rather than heat. Beasts in the shape of grotesque animals are sometimes seen torturing the souls of the dead and huge worms appear to emerge from their bodies. People who report having had these horrible near death experiences also tell of feeling an utter sense of despair and loss. Some mention that a person for whom they did a good deed in life led them back. Others, realizing with horror that they have come to the abyss, have been saved by continuously uttering the name of Jesus Christ. It would be interesting to do follow up studies on those who have had terrible near death experiences to determine if the ordeal changed their lives.

Not everyone believes in hell. Some ask: "How could a loving God send people to everlasting torment." The word to be careful of in the preceding sentence is "send." Hell is a place for those who *choose* not to be with God.

Why is hell always described as being so terrible? I personally had an experience that helps me to understand.

One night in New York City, my brother-in-law and I were walking back to our hotel. We were at the edge of Central Park and I needed to go to the bathroom. I went into the park alone and met a man there who seemed to be in a lookout role. In response to my question, he nodded that the bathroom was further on. Continuing deeper I saw in the darkness the shape of the building and met two men. I don't remember exactly their words, but something about their manner and the deep, sinister tone of their voices frightened me. Suddenly, I had the feeling that if I continued to the bathroom, I would come out without my wallet, or worse. To me, hell might be like that. No good people around, no police protection, and the depraved evil of hardened sinners abusing each other freely in the total absence of law and order. Add Satan.

Discussion questions

1. Why do you suppose Christ talked so much about hell?

2. If there were no laws, no police and no prisons, what might life in your town be like?

3. Do you find it hard to believe that a "good God" would "send" people to hell for all eternity? Explain your answer.

Chapter Nine

Who actually goes there?

God alone fully knows the minds of men. Christ says in Luke 6:37, "Judge not, and ye shall not be judged." We might strongly presume a person like Hitler is in hell, but we are not the judge.

It is clear there is no sin in heaven. Those who wish to go there will have to renounce serious sin. Anyone who does not want to give up a life of sin is a candidate for hell. Those who in their pride will not bend their will to an almighty God are candidates. The words, "Thy will be done," is the fourth line of the Our Father, the prayer Christ taught his disciples. To escape hell seems to require our willingness to submit to the will of God.

Nevertheless, there may be a much more important determinant of who goes to heaven and who goes to hell. Christ himself makes it plain in Matthew, Chapter 25,

"When the Son of Man comes in his glory, and all the angels with him, he will sit upon his glorious throne, and all the nations will be assembled before him. And he will separate them one from another, as a shepherd separates the sheep from the goats. He will place the sheep on his right and the goats on his left. Then the king will say to those on his right, 'Come, you who are blessed by my Father. Inherit the kingdom prepared for you from the foundation of the world. For I was hungry and you gave me drink, a stranger and you welcomed me, naked and you clothed me, ill and you cared for me, in prison and you visited me.' Then the righteous will answer him and say, 'Lord, when did we see you hungry and feed you, or thirsty and give you drink? When did we see you a stranger and welcome you, or naked and clothe you? When did we see you ill or in prison, and visit you?' And the king will say to them in reply, 'Amen, I say to you, whatever you did for one of these least brothers of mine, you did for me.'

Then he will say to those on his left, 'Depart from me, you accursed, into the eternal fire prepared for the devil and his angels. For I was hungry and you gave me no food, I was thirsty and you gave me no drink, a stranger and you gave me no welcome, naked and you gave me no clothing, ill and in prison, and you did not care for me.' Then they will answer and say, 'Lord, when did we see you hungry or thirsty or a stranger or naked or ill or in prison, and not minister to your needs?' He will answer them, 'Amen, I say to you, what you did not do for one of these least ones, you did not do for me.' And these will go off to eternal punishment, but the righteous to eternal life."

This passage, in Christ's own words, makes it quite clear that our willingness to be charitable and to help others in need is the standard God uses to determine our fitness for heaven or hell.

As limited human beings, it is very hard for us to grasp the unlimited love God has for each one of us. If we are honest with ourselves, each of us craves love and appreciation. We can never get enough. We are so frequently disappointed in others and in ourselves. At times, we may even wallow in self-pity. At other times, we may reject love and become bitter, taking perverse pleasure in hurting others because we ourselves have been hurt.

Instead of turning to good people and to God we may and often do turn to addictions, buy things that get us noticed, and put down others to buck up our own low self esteem. These pursuits may help us to feel good for a while, but we remain unsatisfied. We want something more; we want to be appreciated for who we are. Unfortunately, in striving for these heartfelt needs, we often don't know where to turn. Church may be an option, but we may believe that people who go to church are hypocrites. We feel we don't need anyone to help us. We are strong and can tough things out. We don't even need God. Certainly not a god whom we can blame for taking away someone we loved.

But we do need Him. The man who died for us on the cross didn't have to die, but he did—for us. To save us and to show us the love of God. That man is infinitely stronger than you or I. We need Him. We need to accept His love for each one of us. We need to see the God-made beauty in creation and not focus on the negatives. In so doing we can become better persons. We can begin to care about others, because we are not wrapped up in ourselves. We can see joy in our lives—with Jesus.

God does not give up on any of his people. We are all made in His image and likeness. (Genesis 1:26,27) He is constantly reaching out to us, sending His love down upon both the good and the bad. For a few, a deathbed conversion is their final acceptance of a God who all along tried to show them His love. Ultimately, it is not God who gives up on any of his sons and daughters. It is man. God will never turn His back on us, but we have the freedom to turn our back on Him. God has given human beings freedom. He will not take that freedom away. We can choose not to be with Him for eternity. It is our choice. Alternatively, we can choose to enjoy the full extent of God's bounty and love for each of us forever. That is what God wants for us. To share in His love and glory always.

Discussion questions

1. What seems to be Christ's main criteria for who is saved and who is not?

2. Why do you think it might be important from a religious perspective for each of us to have self-esteem?

3. Without being overly modest, what are some of the gifts or talents God has given you?

4. We live in a secular world among many who have little knowledge or understanding of God's love. They may be people we work with, our friends, neighbors and relatives. Because we are Christian, what should they expect from us?

Conclusion

We will never know exactly what heaven is like until we get there. As Paul writes in 1 Corinthians, 2:9:

"Eye has not seen, and ear has not heard,
and what has not entered the human heart,
what God has prepared for those who love him,"

It is quite possible the experience of paradise may be different for different people. According to St. Thomas, a renowned Doctor of the Church, there are different degrees of happiness in heaven depending on the degree of a person's charity.

Another well known saint, St Therese of Lisieux, the "Little Flower,"used the example of two vessels—one a thimble and the other a large glass. Each is filled to the brim so that they can hold no more. In such a way, those most saintly would be filled with bountiful happiness, and the least of those entering paradise would also be filled to the limit of their happiness.

Those of us with faith in God's love, whether Christian, Muslim, Jew or other, know that He calls each of us to be with Him forever in heaven. Despite the fact that our culture seldom mentions an eternal reward, the reality of our future life should not be forgotten. Rather, it should guide our choices and actions each day.

As Jesus said, "What, then, will anyone gain by winning the whole world and forfeiting his life?" Matthew16:26.

www.ingramcontent.com/pod-product-compliance
Lightning Source LLC
Chambersburg PA
CBHW032112040426
42337CB00040B/228